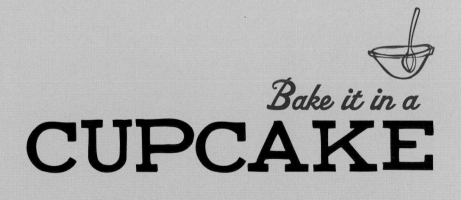

Bake it in a

CUPCAKE

Bake it in a
CUPCAKE
50 treats with a surprise inside

MEGAN SELING

PHOTOGRAPHY BY CLARE BARBOZA

**Andrews McMeel
Publishing, LLC**
Kansas City · Sydney · London

For Other Mom and the Cookie Lady, who put baked goods in my blood, and for Robby, for helping me pick the phyllo dough out of my hair after a particularly interesting cupcake-induced meltdown.

Andrews McMeel Publishing, LLC
an Andrews McMeel Universal company
1130 Walnut Street, Kansas City, Missouri 64106

www.andrewsmcmeel.com | www.bakeitinacake.com

12 13 14 15 16 SHO 10 9 8 7 6 5 4 3 2 1
ISBN: 978-1-4494-2068-0
Library of Congress Control Number: 2012936293

Design and art direction: Kate Basart/Union Pageworks
Photography: Clare Barboza | Food stylist: Helene Dujardin

ATTENTION: SCHOOLS AND BUSINESSES
Andrews McMeel books are available at quantity discounts with bulk purchase for educational, business, or sales promotional use. For information, please e-mail the Andrews McMeel Publishing Special Sales Department: specialsales@amuniversal.com

CONTENTS

INTRODUCTION

You love to bake. Or maybe you just love gawking at the delicious-looking results of someone else's hard work in the kitchen. Either way, this book has something for you: This is a cookbook dedicated to cupcakes and all the delicious things you can bake inside of them.

I grew up in a family of amateur (but terrific) bakers—my great-grandmother was known by neighborhood kids as the Cookie Lady, and my grandma (Hi, Grams!) makes the best oatmeal-raisin cookies you've ever had. But the baking bug didn't bite me until one winter when I went on a holiday cookie-baking binge. I found the act of baking both relaxing and fulfilling, but it wasn't long before I wanted to do more than just follow a recipe. I started small—changing the amount of certain ingredients just to see what would happen, or substituting one cookie mix-in for another based on what I had in my kitchen, but I never got too wild.

Until one spring day, after being inspired by an aisle of 50 percent–off Easter candy, I wondered what would happen if I baked a miniature Cadbury Creme Egg into the center of a cupcake. Duh! Why didn't I think of this before? I grabbed a boxed cake mix, a tub of frosting, and an armload of foil-wrapped chocolate eggs, and rushed home to begin my sweet scientific experiment.

It worked! And friends raved. Thus the idea of *Bake It in a Cupcake* was born. Since the summer of 2010, I've been baking pies into cupcakes, French toast into cheesecakes, and Twix into brownies, and I've posted many of my results on my Web site, www.bakeitinacake.com. Over time, I crafted what I believe to be the perfect cupcake recipe—a slightly heavier cake (page 27) that can hold the candy insides—and whipped up a really simple but oh-so-delicious buttercream frosting base (page 16) which I use on just about everything.

Within these pages there are fifty recipes that make up a collection of creations that will satisfy even the most monstrous sweet tooth. There are even some savory recipes—Chili- and Cheddar-Filled Biscuits (page 102) and Egg-Filled Croissant Cups with Swiss Cheese and Chives (page 101), just to name a couple.

The best part (I bet you thought it couldn't get any better): This is only the beginning. One of the greatest aspects of baking things into other things is that the list of possibilities is literally endless. So at the end of the book I've left some space for you to begin building your own *Bake It in a Cupcake* creations. On page x I have shared some tips so you can learn from my mistakes—and believe me, my kitchen has seen *many* messy mistakes.

Gone are the days where you have to choose cake *or* pie for dessert. With *Bake It in a Cupcake* recipes you can have them both at the same time. As the old saying goes, it's what's on the inside that counts.

BAKING TIPS AND RECOMMENDED TOOLS

You don't need fancy kitchen gadgets or expensive designer cupcake tins to get the results seen within this book. With stuffed goods growing increasingly popular every day, the baking industry has come out with a slew of different gadgets that make it easy to create filled cupcakes—I've seen everything from cupcake corers to spiked muffin tins that supposedly hold your treat in place. You can buy those things if you want, but I did everything in this book using a small collection of easy-to-find items, many of which you probably already have in your kitchen. Here's a list of what this book will ask you to use, as well as a few lessons I've learned along the way. You don't have to take my advice, of course. Get crazy and take a risk. Dive right in and see what happens. That's how this whole thing started, after all.

WHAT YOU WILL NEED (AND SOME STUFF THAT'S NICE TO HAVE)

An electric stand or hand mixer

Two 12-cup (average-size) muffin tins

Two 24-cup (miniature-size) muffin tins

A 1-inch cookie dough scoop

A good, sturdy spatula or wooden spoon

Measuring cups and measuring spoons

Cookie sheets

A rolling pin

Parchment paper

Nonstick baking spray

Mixing bowls

A pastry bag with assorted tips

A sense of adventure and a sweet tooth

WHAT YOU WILL NEED TO KNOW

- As far as I can tell, you cannot bake chewy, fruit-flavored candy like Starbursts, jelly beans, gummy candies, or taffy into a cupcake. I've tried. Believe me, I've tried. Sour Patch Kids are one of my all-time favorites, and I'd love to put them in a cake. But because they're basically just flavored sugar, the softer candies melt and sink to the bottom of the cupcake tins, resulting in an inedible, gooey mess. Such candies are best used as decoration or, if you must do something with those Buttered Popcorn Jelly Bellies, you can melt them down and whip them into frosting.

- Sadly, marshmallows don't work, either. I've tried 'em frozen, I've tried 'em covered in chocolate— I've tried big ones and small ones. Every single time, without fail, the air-filled sugar puffs just dissolve into nothing. They're far too sensitive to heat. If you love marshmallows (Me too!), marshmallow creme works great in frosting (see page 34).

- You *can* bake just about any candy bar into a cupcake. Snickers, Take 5, Whatchamacallit, York Peppermint Patties, Almond Joy, PayDay— they all work wonderfully in both cupcakes and brownies. The heavier candy bars give the best results when baked in the brownie batter, as it's denser, making it harder for the candy to sink.

- If you want to go rogue and bake something into a cake without a recipe (You can do it!), I recommend baking half a pan's worth of cupcakes first, just to make sure your idea works. Now that I say this, it sounds like common sense; but there were several times when I was so excited to try a new idea, and so sure that it was going to work, that I baked off all my cupcake batter in one fell swoop, only to be left with ugly lumps of disappointment and no cupcake batter left to try again. Bake a small batch first, and if it doesn't work, you still have some batter left, so your day isn't a complete waste.

- Be fearless. *I wonder if I can bake a mozzarella stick into a muffin.* There is only one way to find out!

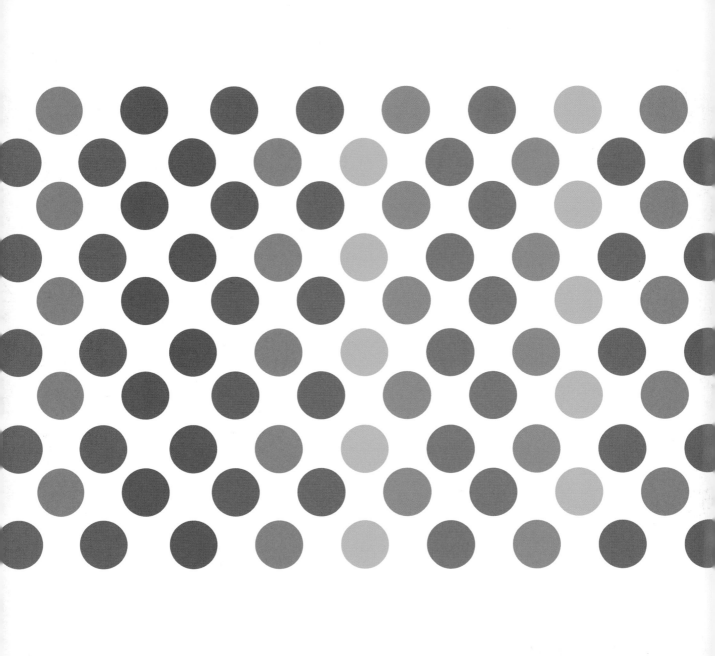

Chapter 1

BAKED GOODS IN A CUPCAKE

Cadbury Creme Eggs were the first candies I baked into a cake, but the first baked good I ever put into a cupcake was a miniature cherry pie. I stood next to the oven, with my fingers crossed tightly, hoping that my seemingly genius idea would actually work—I had to fight the urge to open the oven door every 2 minutes to see how things were coming along. Just over 20 minutes later, voilà! It worked! The mini cherry pie, crust and all, was sitting pretty in the center of the warm chocolate cupcake, just as I imagined it would. And it was absolutely *delicious*.

That was the very moment my new hobby became an obsession. That very day I made a list of all the other pies I could bake into a cupcake—peach, blueberry, blackberry, apple, etc. A list of cookies, cake, and other desserts soon followed. As this chapter proves, just about *any* baked good can be baked successfully inside a cupcake, including miniature pumpkin pies, coconut macaroons, peanut butter blossom cookies, and even baklava. Sure, some of these treats require twice the effort, but all your hard work results in twice the reward, too.

Coconut Macaroon Brownie Cupcakes with Chocolate Ganache

An absolute MUST for anyone who is a fan of Almond Joy candy bars! A moist, homemade macaroon is baked in the center of a rich brownie and, for an extra dose of chocolaty goodness, these brownies are topped with a thick layer of ganache. I sprinkle mine with toasted almond slices, but if you're not feeling like a nut, you can also top them with toasted coconut or even leave them naked.

MAKES 15 CUPCAKES

MACAROONS

1 egg white
1 cup sweetened condensed milk
1 teaspoon vanilla extract
1 (16-ounce) package finely shredded
  unsweetened coconut

BROWNIES

4 ounces unsweetened chocolate, broken or
  chopped into small pieces
¾ cup (1½ sticks) unsalted butter
2 cups granulated sugar
3 large eggs
½ teaspoon salt
1 teaspoon vanilla extract
1 cup unbleached all-purpose flour
¼ cup sliced almonds, or finely shredded
  unsweetened coconut, for garnish (optional)

CHOCOLATE GANACHE

4 ounces semisweet chocolate, broken or
  chopped into small pieces

2 tablespoons heavy cream
1 tablespoon unsalted butter

1. To make the macaroons, preheat the oven to 325°F and line a cookie sheet with parchment paper. In a medium bowl, mix together the egg white, condensed milk, and vanilla. Pour in the coconut and continue to mix until all the coconut is coated evenly. Use a tablespoon or a 1-inch cookie dough scoop to form tight mounds of the mixture and place them on the prepared cookie sheet. Bake for 15 to 20 minutes, until the macaroons are golden brown. The cookies will be fragile when first removed from the oven, so allow them to cool on the pan for at least 10 minutes before moving them to a wire rack. While they finish cooling, make the brownies.

2. To make the brownies, increase the oven temperature to 350°F and line 2 standard muffin tins with 15 paper liners. Place the chocolate and butter in a medium microwave-safe bowl

continued on page 5 ➡

and microwave on high for 90 seconds, stopping halfway through to stir the butter and chocolate together. After 90 seconds, continue to stir the butter and chocolate until all the chocolate chunks have melted completely into the butter. (If you microwave any longer, you risk burning the chocolate, so it's best to be patient and let the chocolate melt slowly while you stir.) Using a wooden spoon, stir in the sugar. It will be thick and grainy, and the sugar should be distributed evenly. Next, stir in the eggs one at a time until the mixture is smooth. Add the salt and vanilla and stir for an additional 20 seconds, until they're both incorporated. Finally, mix in the flour until just combined, taking care not to overstir.

3. Put a heaping tablespoon of brownie batter into each cup in the prepared tins. Place one macaroon in each tin, pressing it gently into the batter, and then top the macaroon with more batter so the top and the sides are completely covered. The tins should be about three-quarters full. Bake the brownies for 23 to 25 minutes, until they have begun to set. Begin checking for doneness at 20 minutes, as ovens vary. You can test by sticking a toothpick into the side of the brownie—if it comes out clean, they're done. Be careful not to overbake, though, or your brownies will be dry. Allow the brownies to cool in the cupcake tins for 10 minutes, then transfer them to a wire rack to cool completely. If you are topping your cupcakes with toasted almonds or coconut,

leave the oven on and spread the nuts out in a single layer on a nongreased baking sheet. Spread the coconut out in a thin layer on a cookie sheet lined with parchment paper. Place them in the oven for about 10 minutes, just until they start to turn a golden brown. Allow them to cool before you use them.

4. To make the ganache, place the chocolate, cream, and butter in a small microwave-safe bowl. Microwave on high in 30-second increments, stirring after each zap. When the mixture is nearly melted, continue to stir until all the chocolate is melted and the cream and butter are completely incorporated. Once the ganache has completely melted, dip the tops of the cooled brownies into the chocolate, allow some excess ganache to drip away, and then place the brownies right side up on a wire rack to allow the ganache to set. Garnish with the toasted almond slices or coconut if you like.

BAKER'S TIP

When making these brownies, you can make the macaroons 2 or 3 days in advance to save time on your baking day. Once the cookies are cooled, store them in an airtight container with wax or parchment paper between layers of cookies to prevent sticking. The macaroons are also delicious on their own, or you can fancy them up by dipping the bottom of each cooled cookie into some melted semisweet or milk chocolate. There isn't a single food in the world that doesn't taste better after being dipped into chocolate.

Banana Pudding Pie Cupcakes with Butterscotch

If you ask me (and I suppose because you're reading this book you technically *did* ask me), you just can't have banana pudding without vanilla wafers; so while the banana pie inside is very important, it's the crumbled vanilla wafers that really make this cupcake as delicious as it is. The butterscotch doesn't hurt, either.

MAKES 24 CUPCAKES

BANANA PUDDING PIES

1 (16-ounce) batch pie crust dough (your favorite recipe or store-bought, enough to make a 2-crust pie)

1 (4.6-ounce) box instant banana pudding, made as directed on the box

CUPCAKES

¾ cup (1½ sticks) unsalted butter, at room temperature

1½ cups granulated sugar

3 large eggs

2 teaspoons vanilla extract

2 teaspoons baking powder

½ teaspoon baking soda

½ teaspoon salt

2½ cups unbleached all-purpose flour

1⅓ cups whole milk

FROSTING

2 tablespoons heavy cream or whole milk

1 cup butterscotch chips

1 cup (2 sticks) unsalted butter, at room temperature

2 cups powdered sugar

1 cup vanilla wafer cookies, crushed, for garnish

24 dried banana chips, for garnish

1. To make the pie shells, preheat the oven to 375°F and lightly grease a 24-cup miniature muffin tin. Use a rolling pin to roll out the pie crust dough on a lightly floured smooth surface so the dough is about ⅛ inch thick. Then use a 2½-inch circular cookie cutter to cut out 24 small circles. Press the dough circles into the muffin tin and bake for 7 to 10 minutes, until the crusts turn golden brown. Remove them from the oven and allow them to cool completely in the tin. Once the pie shells are cool, spoon a tablespoon of the banana pudding into each shell. Set aside.

2. To make the cupcake batter, turn down the oven temperature to 350°F and line 2 standard muffin tins with 24 paper liners. Use a stand mixer fitted with the paddle attachment or a hand mixer on medium speed to combine the butter and sugar for 90 seconds, until fluffy. Add the eggs one at a time, mixing in each egg completely before adding the next. With the mixer on medium-low speed, add the vanilla, baking powder, baking soda, and salt. Turn the mixer up to medium-high speed and mix for an additional 30 seconds, until all the ingredients are well combined. Finally, add the flour, ½ cup at a time, alternately with the milk, ⅓ cup at a time, mixing until each addition is completely incorporated before adding the next. Continue to mix the batter on medium-high speed for 30 seconds, until smooth and creamy.

3. Spoon a heaping tablespoon of batter into each cup in the prepared tins. Place a cooled banana pudding pie into the center of the batter and press it in gently. You don't want the pie to touch the bottom of the tin. Cover the pies with another heaping tablespoon of batter so the top and sides of the mini pie are completely covered and the cup is about three-quarters full. Bake at 350°F for 25 minutes, until the edges and tops of the cupcakes have turned golden brown and the cake springs back when you gently press your finger into the top of it. Allow the cupcakes to cool in the tins for at least 10 minutes before moving to a wire rack to cool completely—they'll be a little fragile at first.

4. To make the frosting, melt the cream and butterscotch chips together in a small microwave-safe bowl for about 45 seconds on high. Stir the mixture until all the chips have melted and place the bowl in the fridge while you prepare the rest of the frosting. Using a stand mixer fitted with the whisk attachment or a hand mixer, whip the butter on medium-high speed for about 30 seconds, until smooth. Whip in the powdered sugar, ½ cup at a time, until the mixture is fluffy. Finally, with the mixer on low, drizzle in the butterscotch chip mixture. (Make sure it has cooled a bit—if it's too hot, it will melt the frosting.) Stop the mixer and scrape down the sides of the bowl, then continue to whip for 30 seconds, until the butterscotch is completely incorporated. Spread or swirl a generous helping of the frosting onto the cupcakes using a spatula or pastry bag (see page 137) and top with some crushed vanilla wafer cookies and a banana chip.

Baklava Honey-Vanilla Cupcakes with Spiced Frosting

This recipe *looks* labor intensive, but it is actually quite simple. While it takes some patience to construct the baklava, the majority of your time is spent waiting for it to bake, and believe me, it is worth the wait. The baklava is sweet and flowery (flavored with just a splash of rose water), which goes wonderfully with the spices in the buttercream.

And should you have any baklava left over, it freezes really well. Just wrap it tightly in plastic wrap and store it in an airtight container for later use (or treat yourself to a snack while you wait for the cupcakes to bake).

MAKES 20 CUPCAKES

BAKLAVA
½ pound assorted nuts (I suggest equal amounts of pistachios, walnuts, and pecans)
1 tablespoon ground cinnamon
1 (16-ounce) package or 26 sheets frozen phyllo dough, thawed
½ cup (1 stick) unsalted butter, softened, plus more for the pan
1 cup water
1 cup granulated sugar
½ cup honey
2 teaspoons vanilla extract
½ teaspoon rose water

CUPCAKES
¾ cup (1½ sticks) unsalted butter, at room temperature
1¼ cups granulated sugar
3 large eggs
2 teaspoons vanilla extract
2 teaspoons baking powder
½ teaspoon baking soda
½ teaspoon salt
2½ cups unbleached all-purpose flour
1 cup whole milk
¼ cup honey

FROSTING
1 cup (2 sticks) unsalted butter, at room temperature
2 cups powdered sugar
1 teaspoon vanilla extract
1 tablespoon ground cinnamon
2 teaspoons freshly grated nutmeg
1 teaspoon ground cloves
2 tablespoons ground pistachios, for garnish

1. To make the baklava, preheat the oven to 350°F and butter a 9-inch square baking pan. Finely chop the nuts by hand or in a food processor. Place them in a medium bowl with the cinnamon; toss, and set aside. Unroll the phyllo dough and cut it in half. Stack the 2 halves and trim off the edges so the dough will fit into the baking pan (if you'd like to save the scraps of phyllo dough for later use, immediately wrap them in plastic and put them in the refrigerator or freezer). Place a damp cloth or paper towel over the stack of dough to keep it from drying out while you work.

2. Place 2 sheets of phyllo dough in the bottom of the pan and brush with a thin, even layer of softened butter. Put 2 more sheets of phyllo dough on top and brush with more butter. Repeat twice more so you have a total of 8 layers of phyllo dough in the pan. Sprinkle a few heaping tablespoons of the nut mixture over the dough in an even layer, taking care to reach all the way to the edges. Put 2 pieces of phyllo dough on top of the nut mixture, brush with butter, and sprinkle with nuts again. Repeat that process 4 more times so you have 5 layers of the nut mixture. To top off the baklava, repeat the first steps—put down 2 layers of phyllo dough, brush with butter, top with 2 more layers of dough, more butter, until you have 6 to 8 sheets layered on top. Brush the very top layer with some butter.

3. Use a very sharp knife to cut the pan of baklava into 20 equal-size pieces. Bake for about 50 minutes, until the baklava has turned a deep golden brown. While the baklava bakes, make the syrup by heating the water and sugar in a small saucepan over medium heat. Once all the sugar is dissolved, add the honey, vanilla, and rose water. Bring the liquid to a boil, stirring occasionally, then decrease the heat to low and simmer for 25 minutes. When the baklava is done, remove it from the oven and, while it is still very hot, pour the syrup over it. Allow it to cool in the pan while you make the cupcake batter.

4. To make the cupcakes, line 2 standard muffin tins with 20 paper liners. Use a stand mixer fitted with the paddle attachment or a hand mixer on medium speed to combine the butter and sugar for 90 seconds, until fluffy. Add the eggs, one at a time, mixing in each egg completely before adding the next. With the mixer on medium-low speed, add the vanilla, baking powder, baking soda, and salt. Use a spatula to scrape down the sides of the bowl, increase the speed to medium-high, and mix for an additional 30 seconds, until all the ingredients are well combined. Finally, add the flour, ½ cup at a time, alternately with the milk, ⅓ cup at a time, mixing until each addition is completely incorporated before adding the next. Scrape down the sides of the bowl again, then add the honey and continue to mix the batter on medium-high speed for 30 seconds, until smooth and creamy.

continued on page 11 ⇒

BAKED GOODS IN A CUPCAKE

9

5. Spoon a heaping tablespoon of batter into each cup in the prepared tins. Place a cooled piece of baklava into the center of the batter and press it gently toward the bottom. Cover the baklava with another heaping tablespoon of batter so the top and sides are completely covered and the cup is about three-quarters full. Bake at 350°F for about 25 minutes, until the edges and tops of the cupcakes have turned golden brown and the cake springs back when you gently press your finger into the top of it. Allow the cupcakes to cool in the tins for at least 10 minutes before moving them to a wire rack to cool completely.

6. To make the frosting, whip the butter for about 30 seconds with a stand mixer fitted with the whisk attachment or a hand mixer on medium speed. Add the powdered sugar, ½ cup at a time, whipping on medium-high speed until fluffy. Add the vanilla, cinnamon, nutmeg, and cloves and whip until just combined. Pipe or spread the frosting on top of the cooled cupcakes. Personally, I like to frost these cupcakes with a more rustic finish, which goes well with the ruffled layers in the baklava, so don't worry about making them look perfect. Top the finished cupcakes with a sprinkling of ground pistachios.

Coconut Macaroon Key Lime Cupcakes with Key Lime Frosting

My husband (and official cupcake taster) makes the best key lime pie you will ever eat. It's not surprising, since his grandparents spent the first half of their marriage as lime farmers in Florida. Since we always have a bottle of key lime juice in our fridge, one afternoon I dumped a bunch of it into some vanilla cupcake batter, shoved a macaroon inside, and—surprise!—the results were tangy and incredibly delicious. The macaroons can be made 2 to 3 days in advance (see page 9).

MAKES 20 CUPCAKES

MACAROONS
1 egg white
1 cup sweetened condensed milk
1 teaspoon vanilla extract
1 (16-ounce) package finely shredded unsweetened coconut

CUPCAKES
3/4 cup (1 1/2 sticks) unsalted butter, at room temperature
1 1/2 cups granulated sugar
3 large eggs
2 teaspoons vanilla extract
2 teaspoons baking powder
1/2 teaspoon baking soda
1/4 teaspoon salt
2 1/2 cups unbleached all-purpose flour
1 1/3 cups whole milk
1/4 cup key lime juice (fresh or bottled)
1 cup finely shredded unsweetened coconut, or more to taste, for garnish

FROSTING
1 cup (2 sticks) unsalted butter, at room temperature
2 cups powdered sugar
1/4 cup key lime juice (fresh or bottled)

1. To make the macaroons, preheat the oven to 325°F and line a cookie sheet with parchment paper. In a medium bowl, mix together the egg white, condensed milk, and vanilla. Pour in the coconut and continue to mix until all the coconut is coated evenly. Use a tablespoon or a 1-inch kitchen scoop to form tight mounds of the mixture and place them on the prepared cookie sheet. Bake for 15 to 20 minutes, until the macaroons are golden brown. The cookies will be fragile when first removed from the oven, so allow them to cool on the pan for at least 10 minutes before moving them to a wire rack. While they finish cooling, make the cupcakes.

2. To make the cupcakes, turn the oven up to 350°F and line 2 standard muffin tins with 20 paper liners. Use a stand mixer fitted with the paddle attachment or a hand mixer on medium speed to combine the butter and sugar for 90 seconds, until fluffy. Add the eggs, one at a time, mixing in each egg completely before adding the next. With the mixer on medium-low speed, add the vanilla, baking powder, baking soda, and salt. Turn the mixer up to medium-high speed and mix for an additional 30 seconds, until all the ingredients are well combined. Finally, add the flour, ½ cup at a time, alternately with the milk, ⅓ cup at at a time, mixing until each addition is completely incorporated before adding the next. Pour in the lime juice and continue to mix the batter on medium-high speed for 30 seconds, until smooth and creamy.

3. Put a heaping tablespoon of batter into each cup in the prepared tins. Place a macaroon in each tin, pressing it gently into the batter, and then top the macaroon with more batter so the top and the sides are completely covered. The cupcake tins should be about three-quarters full. Bake for about 25 minutes, until the edges and tops of the cupcakes have turned golden brown and the cake springs back when you gently press your finger into the top of it. Allow the cupcakes to cool in the tins for at least 10 minutes before moving to a wire rack to cool completely. If you are using toasted coconut as a garnish, leave the oven on and spread the coconut out in a thin layer on a cookie sheet that has been lined with parchment paper. Place in the oven for about 10 minutes, until the coconut has started to turn golden brown.

4. For the frosting, whip the butter for about 30 seconds with a stand mixer fitted with the whisk attachment or a hand mixer on medium speed. Add the powdered sugar, ½ cup at a time, whipping on medium-high speed until fluffy. With the mixer on medium speed, drizzle in the lime juice and continue to whip on medium-high speed until fluffy. Give it a taste and add more lime juice if desired. If you'd like, top each cupcake with a generous pinch of toasted coconut.

Seven-Layer Bar Brownie Cupcakes

Layer one: butter. Layer two: graham cracker crumbs. Layer three: chocolate chips. Layer four: butterscotch chips. Layer five: coconut. Layer six: condensed milk. Layer seven: pecans. Layer awesome: PUT IT IN A CUPCAKE.

MAKES 15 CUPCAKES

SEVEN-LAYER BAR COOKIES
4 tablespoons (½ stick) butter, melted
1 cup graham cracker crumbs
1 cup chocolate chips
1 cup butterscotch chips
1 cup shredded sweetened coconut
1 cup chopped pecans
1 (14-ounce) can condensed milk

BROWNIES
4 ounces unsweetened chocolate, broken or chopped into small pieces
¾ cup (1½ sticks) unsalted butter
2 cups granulated sugar
3 large eggs
½ teaspoon salt
1 teaspoon vanilla extract
1 cup unbleached all-purpose flour

FROSTING
2 sticks (1 cup) unsalted butter, at room temperature
2 cups powdered sugar
2 teaspoons vanilla extract
2 tablespoons whole milk, if needed
Dark or milk chocolate shavings, for garnish

1. To make the seven-layer bars, preheat the oven to 350°F and spray a 9-inch square baking pan with nonstick cooking spray. Stir the melted butter and graham cracker crumbs together until all the crumbs are moist with butter. Press them into the bottom of the prepared pan. Pour the chocolate chips over the graham cracker crust in an even layer. Do the same with the butterscotch chips, coconut, and pecans. Pour the condensed milk over the ingredients and bake for about 25 minutes, until the edges are bubbling and the coconut is starting to turn golden brown. Allow to cool completely before cutting.

2. To make the cupcakes, line 2 standard muffin tins with 15 paper liners. Place the chocolate and butter in a medium microwave-safe bowl and microwave on high for 90 seconds, stopping halfway through to stir the butter and chocolate together. After 90 seconds, continue to stir the butter and chocolate until all the chocolate chunks have melted completely into the butter. (If you microwave any longer, you risk burning the chocolate, so it's best to be patient and let the chocolate melt slowly while you stir.) Using a wooden spoon, stir in the granulated sugar. It will be thick and grainy, and the sugar should be distributed evenly throughout. Next, stir in the eggs one at a time until the mixture is smooth. Add the salt and vanilla and stir for an additional 20 seconds, until they're both incorporated. Finally, mix in the flour until just combined, taking care not to overstir.

3. Cut the cookie bars into 16 equal pieces. (Since you will have one left over, it's okay to sneak a snack.) Using a 1-inch scoop, spoon the brownie batter into the prepared tins. Press a seven-layer cookie into each cup and cover with more brownie batter so the tins are about three-quarters full. Bake for about 25 minutes, or until the brownies have set. (Take care not to overbake or your brownies could be quite dry.) Allow the brownies to cool in the tins for 10 minutes before transferring to a wire rack to finish cooling.

4. For the frosting, whip the butter for about 30 seconds with a stand mixer fitted with the whisk attachment or a hand mixer on medium speed. Add the powdered sugar, ½ cup at a time, whipping on medium-high speed until fluffy. Add the vanilla and whip until just combined. If the frosting is too thick, add the milk and whip on high for 20 seconds, until the frosting is fluffy. Pipe or spread the frosting on top of the cooled cupcakes (see page 137) and sprinkle with chocolate shavings.

Cherry Pie Dark Chocolate Cupcakes with Vanilla Bean Frosting

While it's nearly impossible for me to answer the oft-asked question, "Which cupcake is your favorite?" the cherry pie–stuffed chocolate cupcakes, the first pie-stuffed cupcakes I ever baked, are most certainly in my top five. Miniature cherry pies overflowing with slightly tart cherry filling, nestled in a rich chocolate cupcake topped with vanilla bean buttercream? I can't imagine ever wanting anything more from a cupcake.

MAKES 24 CUPCAKES

CHERRY PIES

2 (16-ounce) batches pie crust dough (your favorite recipe or store-bought, enough to make 2 two-crust pies)

1 cup cherry pie filling

CUPCAKES

4 ounces unsweetened chocolate, broken or chopped into small pieces

1⅓ cups plus 2 tablespoons whole milk

¾ cup (1½ sticks) unsalted butter, at room temperature

1½ cups granulated sugar

3 large eggs

2 teaspoons vanilla extract

2 teaspoons baking powder

½ teaspoon baking soda

¼ teaspoon salt

½ cup unsweetened cocoa powder

2½ cups unbleached all-purpose flour

FROSTING

1 cup (2 sticks) unsalted butter, at room temperature

2 cups powdered sugar

Seeds from ½ vanilla bean (see page 63)

2 tablespoons whole milk, if needed

24 maraschino cherries, for garnish

1. To make the mini cherry pies, preheat the oven to 375°F and grease a 24-cup miniature muffin tin. Use a rolling pin to roll out the pie crust dough on a lightly floured smooth surface until the dough is about ⅛ inch thick. Then use a 2½-inch circular cookie cutter to cut out 48 small circles.

2. Press the dough circles into the prepared tin and fill them three-quarters full of cherry pie filling. Top each pie with another dough circle, sealing the pies by pinching the edges of the bottom crust to the top crust. Use a sharp knife

continued on page 18 →

to cut a small X into the top of each pie. Bake the pies for 10 to 12 minutes, until the edges of the crust have browned. They may overflow a bit, and that's okay. They don't have to look perfect since they're going into a cupcake! Allow the pies to cool for 10 minutes in the tin and then carefully transfer them to a wire rack to finish cooling while you mix the cupcake batter.

3. To make the cupcakes, turn the oven temperature down to 350°F. Line 2 standard muffin tins with 24 paper liners. Place the chocolate and 2 tablespoons of the milk in a small microwave-safe bowl and microwave for 20 seconds on high. Stir and microwave for another 20 seconds. Stir the mixture until the chocolate has melted completely and the cream is fully incorporated. Place the bowl in the refrigerator so it can cool while you prepare the rest of the cupcake batter. Use a stand mixer fitted with the paddle attachment or a hand mixer on medium speed to combine the butter and sugar for 90 seconds, until fluffy. Add the eggs, one at a time, mixing in each egg completely before adding the next. Use a spatula to scrape down the sides of the bowl. Then, with the mixer on medium-low speed, add the vanilla, baking powder, baking soda, and salt. Add the cocoa powder. Turn the mixer up to medium-high speed and mix for an additional 30 seconds, until all the ingredients are well combined. Scrape down the sides of the bowl and then add the flour, ½ cup at

a time, alternately with the milk, ⅓ cup at a time, mixing until each addition is completely incorporated before adding the next. Finally, with the mixer on medium-high, drizzle in the cooled chocolate mixture. Continue to mix the batter on medium-high speed for 30 seconds, until smooth and creamy.

4. Spoon a heaping tablespoon of batter into each cup in the prepared tins. Place a cooled cherry pie into the center of the batter and press it gently toward the bottom. Cover the pie with another heaping tablespoon of batter so the top and sides are completely covered and the cup is about three-quarters full. Bake for about 25 minutes, until the edges and tops of the cupcakes have set and the cake springs back when you gently press your finger into the top of it. Allow the cupcakes to cool in the tins for at least 10 minutes before moving to a wire rack to cool completely.

5. For the frosting, whip the butter for about 30 seconds with a stand mixer fitted with the whisk attachment or a hand mixer on medium speed. Add the powdered sugar, ½ cup at a time, whipping on medium-high speed until fluffy. Add the vanilla seeds and whip until just combined. If the frosting is too thick, add the milk and whip on high for 20 seconds. Pipe or spread the frosting on top of the cooled cupcakes (see page 137). Top each cupcake with a cherry.

Lemon Bar Vanilla Cupcakes with Fresh Raspberry Frosting

Behold, one of the most popular *Bake It in a Cupcake* creations. The tart lemony center and sweet raspberry top remind me of pink lemonade, so these are especially perfect for summertime. To make them even easier to prepare, I use a boxed lemon bar mix. (I'm not ashamed of taking short-cuts.) But if you have your own lemon bar recipe, feel free to whip up a batch of those, instead. And if you want to make these treats in the dead of winter, the frosting is just as easy to make using frozen raspberries in place of fresh.

MAKES 20 CUPCAKES

CUPCAKES

¾ cup (1½ sticks) unsalted butter, at room
    temperature
1½ cups granulated sugar
3 large eggs
2 teaspoons vanilla extract
2 teaspoons baking powder
½ teaspoon baking soda
¼ teaspoon salt
2½ cups unbleached all-purpose flour
1⅓ cups whole milk
1 batch lemon bars baked in a 9-inch square pan,
    cooled and cut into 20 pieces

FROSTING

1 cup fresh or thawed frozen raspberries
1 cup (2 sticks) unsalted butter, at room
    temperature
2 cups powdered sugar
1 teaspoon vanilla extract
2 tablespoons whole milk, if needed
Additional raspberries or candied lemon zest,
    for garnish

1. To make the cupcakes, preheat the oven to 350°F and line 2 standard muffin tins with 20 paper liners. Use a stand mixer fitted with the paddle attachment or a hand mixer on medium speed to combine the butter and sugar for 90 seconds, until fluffy. Add the eggs, one at a time, mixing in each egg completely before adding the next. With the mixer on medium-low speed, add the vanilla, baking powder, baking soda, and salt. Turn the mixer up to

continued on page 21

medium-high speed and mix for an additional 30 seconds, until all the ingredients are well combined. Add the flour, ½ cup at a time, alternately with the milk, ⅓ cup at a time, mixing until each addition is completely incorporated before adding the next. Continue to mix the batter on medium-high speed for 30 seconds, until smooth and creamy.

2. Spoon a heaping tablespoon of batter into each cup of the prepared tins. Place a lemon bar in the center of the batter and press it gently toward the bottom. Cover the lemon bar with another heaping tablespoon of batter so the top and sides are completely covered and the cup is about three-quarters full. Bake for about 25 minutes, until the edges and tops of the cupcakes have turned golden brown and the cake springs back when you gently press your finger into the top of it. Allow the cupcakes to cool in the tins for at least 10 minutes before moving to a wire rack to cool completely.

3. For the frosting, purée the raspberries in a blender or food processor and then run the raspberry purée through a cheesecloth or fine-mesh strainer to remove all the seeds. Throw the seeds away and set the raspberry purée aside. Next, whip the butter for about 30 seconds with a stand mixer fitted with the whisk attachment or a hand mixer on medium speed. Add the powdered sugar, ½ cup at a time, whipping on medium-high speed until fluffy. Add the vanilla and raspberry purée and whip until just combined. The raspberry juice might cause the frosting to get thick. If so, add the milk and whip on high speed until the frosting is smooth and fluffy. If the frosting is too runny, add a little more powdered sugar. Pipe or spread the frosting on top of the cooled cupcakes (see page 137) and garnish with a raspberry and/or some candied lemon zest.

Coconut Cream Key Lime Cupcakes with Toasted Coconut Frosting

A few recipes in this book take advantage of the amazing flavor equation that is coconut plus lime, but if we're going to be honest (and new friendships like ours are built on honesty), this is my favorite one. The cool, creamy coconut pudding center is simply incredible when balanced with the tart lime cake. Just don't tell the Coconut Macaroon Key Lime Cupcakes on page 12, okay? They'll never forgive me.

MAKES 24 CUPCAKES

COCONUT CREAM PIES
1 (16-ounce) batch pie crust dough (your favorite recipe or store-bought, enough for a 2-crust pie)
1 (4.6-ounce) box instant coconut pudding, made as directed on the box

CUPCAKES
¾ cup (1½ sticks) unsalted butter, at room temperature
1½ cups granulated sugar
3 large eggs
2 teaspoons vanilla extract
2 teaspoons baking powder
½ teaspoon baking soda
¼ teaspoon salt
2½ cups unbleached all-purpose flour
1⅓ cups whole milk
¼ cup key lime juice (fresh or bottled)
1 cup finely shredded unsweetened coconut flakes

FROSTING
1 cup (2 sticks) unsalted butter, at room temperature
½ cup coconut cream
2 cups powdered sugar

1. To make the pie shells, preheat the oven to 375°F and lightly grease 24 cups in a miniature muffin tin. Use a rolling pin to roll out the pie crust dough on a lightly floured smooth surface so the dough is about ⅛ inch thick and then use a 2½-inch circular cookie cutter to cut out 24 small circles. Press the dough circles into the prepared tin and bake for 7 to 10 minutes, until the crusts turn golden brown. Remove them from the oven and allow them to cool completely in the tin. Once the pie shells are cool, spoon a tablespoon of the coconut pudding into each shell. Set aside.

2. To make the cupcakes, turn the oven down to 350°F and line 2 standard muffin tins with 24 paper liners. Use a stand mixer fitted with the paddle attachment or a hand mixer on medium speed to combine the butter and sugar together for 90 seconds, until fluffy. Add the eggs, one at a time, mixing in each egg completely before adding the next. With the mixer on medium-low speed, add the vanilla, baking powder, baking soda, and salt. Turn the mixer up to medium-high speed and mix for an additional 30 seconds, until all the ingredients are well combined. Finally, add the flour, ½ cup at a time, alternately with the milk, ⅓ cup at a time, mixing until each addition is fully incorporated before adding the next. Pour in the lime juice and continue to mix the batter on medium-high speed for 30 seconds, until smooth and creamy.

3. Spoon a heaping tablespoon of batter into each cup in the prepared muffin tins. Place a cooled coconut pudding pie into the center of the batter and press it gently. You don't want the pie to touch the bottom of the tin. Cover the pies with another heaping tablespoon of batter so the top and sides of the mini pie are completely covered and the cup is about three-quarters full. Bake at 350°F for 25 minutes, until the edges and tops of the cupcakes have turned golden brown and the cake springs back when you gently press your finger into the top of it. Allow the cupcakes to cool in the tin for at least 10 minutes before moving to a wire rack to cool completely. If you are using toasted coconut as a garnish, leave the oven on and spread the coconut out in a thin layer on a cookie sheet that has been lined with parchment paper. Place in the oven for about 10 minutes, until the coconut has started to turn golden brown.

4. To make the frosting, use a stand mixer fitted with the whisk attachment or a hand mixer to cream together the butter and coconut cream until the mixture is smooth. Whip in the powdered sugar, ½ cup at a time, until the mixture is fluffy. Spread or swirl a generous helping of the frosting onto the cupcakes using a spatula or pastry bag (see page 137) and top with toasted coconut.

Snickerdoodle Chocolate Cupcakes with Hot Chocolate Frosting

My favorite cookie? Easy. The snickerdoodle. Few things are better than a plate of warm cinnamon- and sugar-coated snickerdoodles, and now that experience comes in the form of a cupcake. There are no fewer than 8,000 snickerdoodle recipes in the world, so I leave it to you to pick your favorite. Martha Stewart has a great one, for example. For these cupcakes, just mix up the dough of your favorite snickerdoodle recipe, use a 1-inch cookie scoop to scoop the dough into balls, roll the dough in some cinnamon sugar, and bake them in your mini muffin tin. That way you'll ensure the cookies will be small enough to fit into your cupcakes. Neat, huh?

MAKES 22 CUPCAKES

CUPCAKES

4 ounces unsweetened chocolate, broken or
  chopped into small pieces
1⅓ cups plus 2 tablespoons whole milk
¾ cup (1½ sticks) unsalted butter, at room
  temperature
1½ cups granulated sugar
3 large eggs
2 teaspoons vanilla extract
2 teaspoons baking powder
½ teaspoon baking soda
¼ teaspoon salt
½ cup unsweetened cocoa powder
2½ cups unbleached all-purpose flour
22 snickerdoodle cookies, baked in a miniature
  muffin tin

FROSTING

½ cup powdered hot chocolate mix
1 tablespoon milk
1 cup (2 sticks) unsalted butter, at room
  temperature
1 (7-ounce) jar marshmallow creme
2 cups powdered sugar

1. To make the cupcakes, preheat the oven to 350°F and line 2 standard muffin tins with 22 paper liners. Place the chocolate and 2 tablespoons of the milk in a small microwave-safe bowl and microwave for 20 seconds on high. Stir and microwave for another 20 seconds. Stir the mixture until the chocolate has completely melted and the cream is fully incorporated. Place the bowl in the refrigerator so it can cool while you prepare the rest of the cupcake batter. Use a stand mixer fitted

with the paddle attachment or a hand mixer on medium speed to combine the butter and sugar for 90 seconds, until fluffy. Add the eggs, one at a time, mixing in each egg completely before adding the next. Use a spatula to scrape down the sides of the bowl. Then, with the mixer on medium-low speed, add the vanilla, baking powder, baking soda, and salt. Add the cocoa powder. Turn the mixer up to medium-high speed and mix for an additional 30 seconds, until all the ingredients are well combined. Scrape down the sides of the bowl. Add the flour, ½ cup at a time, alternately with the remaining 1⅓ cups milk, ⅓ cup at a time, mixing until each addition is fully incorporated before adding the next. Finally, with the mixer on medium-high, drizzle in the cooled chocolate mixture. Continue to mix the batter on medium-high speed for another 30 seconds. It should be smooth and creamy.

2. Spoon a heaping tablespoon of batter into each cup in the prepared tins. Place a cooled snickerdoodle cookie into the center of the batter and press it gently toward the bottom. Cover the cookie with another heaping tablespoon of batter so the top and sides are completely covered and the cup is about three-quarters full. Bake at 350°F for about 25 minutes, until the edges and tops of the cupcakes have set and the cake springs back when you gently press your finger into the top of it. Allow the cupcakes to cool in the tins for at least 10 minutes before moving to a wire rack to cool completely.

3. To make the frosting, whisk the hot chocolate mix and milk together until there are no lumps. Set aside. Whip the butter and marshmallow creme together for about 30 seconds with a stand mixer fitted with the whisk attachment or a hand mixer on medium speed. Add the powdered sugar, ½ cup at a time, whipping on medium-high speed until fluffy. With the mixer on medium speed, slowly drizzle in the hot chocolate mixture. Stop once or twice to scrape down the sides of the bowl and ensure all the ingredients are getting incorporated. Once the frosting is fluffy, pipe or spread the frosting on top of the cooled cupcakes (see page 137).

Cyclops Cookie Cupcakes with Peanut Butter Chocolate Frosting

Peanut butter blossom cookies (or cyclops cookies, as they were called in my house growing up) were such a fun cookie to make as a kid. I loved pressing a chocolate kiss into the warm, freshly baked peanut butter cookie. When these cookies are baked into the center of a vanilla cupcake, they take on a whole new identity—cut the cupcake in half and the cookies look like little flying saucers! Only you'll be taking these extraterrestrial treats directly to your tummy instead of your leader.

MAKES 22 CUPCAKES

PEANUT BUTTER BLOSSOM COOKIES
½ cup plus ¼ cup granulated sugar
4 tablespoons (½ stick) unsalted butter
¼ cup crunchy peanut butter
¼ cup light brown sugar, packed
1 egg
1 teaspoon vanilla extract
1 tablespoon milk
1 cup unbleached all-purpose flour
½ teaspoon baking powder
¼ teaspoon salt
⅛ teaspoon baking soda
22 chocolate kisses

CUPCAKES
¾ cup (1½ sticks) unsalted butter, at room temperature
1½ cups granulated sugar
3 large eggs
2 teaspoons vanilla extract
2 teaspoons baking powder
½ teaspoon baking soda
¼ teaspoon salt
2½ cups unbleached all-purpose flour
1⅓ cups whole milk

FROSTING
1 cup (2 sticks) unsalted butter, at room temperature
½ cup smooth or crunchy peanut butter
2 cups powdered sugar
3 tablespoons unsweetened cocoa powder
2 tablespoons whole milk
¼ cup salted peanuts, chopped

1. To make the cookies, preheat the oven to 350°F. Pour ½ cup of the granulated sugar onto a plate and set aside. Using a stand mixer fitted with the paddle attachment or a hand mixer on medium speed, combine the butter, peanut butter, remaining ¼ cup granulated sugar, and brown sugar for 60 seconds, until fluffy.

continued on page 28 ⇒

2. Add the egg, vanilla, and milk and beat on medium-high speed for an additional 15 to 20 seconds, until all the ingredients are incorporated. Finally, add the flour, baking powder, salt, and baking soda and beat on medium speed for 30 seconds, or until the dough is well mixed. Form pieces of the dough into 1-inch balls, roll in the plate of sugar so the balls are completely coated in granulated sugar, and then place them on a cookie sheet lined with parchment paper 2 inches apart. Bake for 12 to 15 minutes, until the cookies are golden brown. As soon as you remove the cookies from the oven, place an unwrapped chocolate kiss in the center of each cookie, but don't press too hard, because you want the base of the cookie to be small enough to fit into your cupcake tin. Allow the cookies to cool on the cookie sheet for 10 minutes before transferring to a wire rack to finish cooling.

3. To make the cupcakes, line 2 standard muffin tins with 22 paper liners. Use a stand mixer fitted with the paddle attachment or a hand mixer on medium speed to combine the butter and sugar for 90 seconds, until fluffy. Add the eggs, one at a time, mixing in each egg completely before adding the next. With the mixer on medium-low speed, add the vanilla, baking powder, baking soda, and salt. Turn the mixer up to medium-high speed and mix for an additional 30 seconds, until all the ingredients are well combined. Finally, add the flour, ½ cup

at a time, alternately with the milk, ⅓ cup at a time, mixing until each addition is fully incorporated before adding the next. Continue to mix the batter on medium-high speed for 30 seconds, until smooth and creamy.

4. Spoon a heaping tablespoon of batter into each cup in the prepared tins. Place a cookie in the center of the batter and press it gently toward the bottom. Cover the cookie with another heaping tablespoon of batter so the top and sides are completely covered and the cup is about three-quarters full. (The tip of the chocolate kiss might stick out of the batter, which is okay.) Bake at 350°F for about 22 minutes, until the edges and tops of the cupcakes have turned golden brown and the cake springs back when you gently press your finger into the top of it. Allow the cupcakes to cool in the tins for at least 10 minutes before moving to a wire rack to cool completely.

5. For the frosting, whip the butter and peanut butter together for about 30 seconds with a stand mixer fitted with the whisk attachment or a hand mixer on medium speed. Add the powdered sugar, ½ cup at a time, whipping on medium-high speed until fluffy. Add the cocoa powder and milk and whip for an additional 20 seconds, until the frosting is smooth and fluffy. Pipe or spread the frosting on top of the cooled cupcakes (see page 137) and top them with a pinch of chopped peanuts.

Boston Cream Puff Pie Cupcakes with Chocolate Ganache

Boston cream pie is one of the world's most perfect desserts—chocolate ganache, creamy custard, and cake. What's not to love? Well, now you can have all the greatness of a Boston cream pie in the much more manageable (and transportable) cupcake form. And if you're in a rush, you can buy pre-made cream puffs, which are available in the freezer section of many grocery stores. Just make sure they're mini size so they'll fit into your cupcake tins.

MAKES 20 CUPCAKES

CUSTARD
½ cup granulated sugar
¾ cup heavy whipping cream
¾ cup half-and-half
½ vanilla bean (see Baker's Tip on page 63)
3 large egg yolks

CREAM PUFFS
½ cup water
4 tablespoons (½ stick) unsalted butter
½ cup unbleached all-purpose flour
Pinch of salt
2 large eggs

CUPCAKES
¾ cup (1½ sticks) unsalted butter, at room temperature
1½ cups granulated sugar
3 large eggs
2 teaspoons vanilla extract
2 teaspoons baking powder

½ teaspoon baking soda
½ teaspoon salt
2 ½ cups unbleached all-purpose flour
1⅓ cups whole milk

CHOCOLATE GANACHE
4 ounces semisweet chocolate, broken or chopped into small pieces
2 tablespoons heavy cream
1 tablespoon unsalted butter

1. To make the custard, place the sugar, cream, and half-and-half in a small saucepan. Split the vanilla bean lengthwise and scrape the seeds into the saucepan. Add the vanilla bean. Warm the cream over medium heat for 5 to 7 minutes, stirring constantly with a whisk. Do not let the mixture boil; it should just be warm to the touch. Remove the saucepan from the heat. Place the egg yolks in a medium bowl and scramble them lightly with a fork. Slowly

continued on page 30 ➡

add 1 cup of the warm cream mixture, whisking. This will temper the eggs and keep the warm milk from cooking the eggs. (You don't want scrambled custard.) Pour the egg and cream mixture from the bowl into the saucepan with the rest of the warm cream and put the saucepan back over medium heat. Whisk it constantly until it begins to thicken, 7 to 10 minutes. Once the mixture is thick, remove it from the heat. Place a fine-mesh strainer or cheesecloth over a medium bowl and strain the custard through it to remove any lumps and the vanilla bean. It will continue to thicken as it cools. Cool the custard completely while you make the pastry shells.

2. To make the cream puffs, preheat the oven to 425°F and line 2 cookie sheets with parchment paper. Boil the water and butter together in a small saucepan over medium-high heat. Once the mixture is boiling, add the flour and salt, stirring constantly with a spoon. The mixture will almost immediately begin to thicken. Keep stirring while the mixture pulls away from the sides of the pan and forms a ball. Continue to stir for another minute or two—you want to remove excess moisture from the dough. Transfer the dough to the bowl of your stand mixer or a mixing bowl and, using the paddle attachment or a hand mixer, beat in the eggs, one at a time, on medium-high speed. Drop heaping teaspoons of the dough onto the prepared cookie sheets and bake for 20 minutes, until a deep golden brown and completely dry inside. Allow the puffs to cool completely on a wire rack before using a pastry bag or squeeze bottle to fill them with custard. (I don't recommend cutting open the pastry shell to fill them—you want to make as small an incision as possible to help keep all the custard in the shell as the cream puff bakes.) Set them aside while you make the cupcakes. (You'll probably have extra—you've earned a treat.)

3. To make the cupcakes, turn the oven temperature down to 350°F and line 2 standard muffin tins with 20 paper liners. Use a stand mixer fitted with the paddle attachment or a hand mixer on medium speed to combine the butter and sugar for 90 seconds, until fluffy. Add the eggs, one at a time, mixing in each egg completely before adding the next. With the mixer on medium-low speed, add the vanilla, baking powder, baking soda, and salt. Turn the mixer up to medium-high speed and mix for an additional 30 seconds, until all the ingredients are well combined. Finally, add the flour, ½ cup at a time, alternately with the milk, ⅓ cup at a time, mixing until each addition is fully incorporated before adding the next. Continue to mix the batter on medium-high speed for 30 seconds, until smooth and creamy.

4. Spoon a heaping tablespoon of batter into each cup in the prepared tins. Place a cream puff in the center of the batter and press it gently toward the bottom. Cover the puff with another heaping tablespoon of batter so the top and sides are completely covered and the cup is about three-quarters full. Bake for 23 to 25 minutes, until the edges and tops of the cupcakes have turned golden brown and the cake springs back when you gently press your finger into the top of it. Allow the cupcakes to cool in the tins for at least 10 minutes before moving to a wire rack to cool completely.

5. To make the ganache, place the chocolate, cream, and butter in a small microwave-safe bowl. Microwave on high in 30-second increments, stirring after each zap. When the mixture is nearly melted, continue to stir until all the chocolate and the cream and butter are completely incorporated. Once the ganache has completely melted, either pour some of the ganache over the top of the cupcakes or dip the tops of the cupcakes into the chocolate, allow some excess ganache to drip away, and then place the cupcakes back on a wire rack to allow the ganache to set.

The Cheesecuppie Cake: The Ultimate Dessert

You've seen the Turducken, right? It's the infamous dish where a chicken is stuffed into a duck that's stuffed into a turkey and then roasted. Well, meet the Cheesecuppie, the dessert version of the Turducken! It has miniature pies baked into cupcakes baked into a full-size cheesecake. You can use just about any cupcake recipe in this book for the cupcakes inside, but I especially love it with cherry pie–stuffed chocolate cupcakes, which you can find on page 16.

MAKES 1 (9-INCH) CHEESECAKE

1 cup graham cracker crumbs
4 tablespoons (½ stick) unsalted butter, melted
3 (8-ounce) packages cream cheese, at room temperature
3 eggs
1½ cups granulated sugar
2 tablespoons vanilla extract
8 unfrosted Cherry Pie Dark Chocolate Cupcakes (page 16)
1 (21-ounce) can cherry pie filling

1. Preheat the oven to 325°F. Put the graham cracker crumbs in a small bowl and mix in the melted butter until the crumbs are moist. Press the crumb mixture evenly into the bottom of a 9-inch springform pan and set aside.

2. To make the cheesecake batter, use a stand mixer fitted with the paddle attachment or a hand mixer to whip the cream cheese on medium speed for 30 seconds, until creamy and smooth. Add the eggs, one at a time, mixing in each egg completely before adding the next. Scrape down the sides of the bowl and whip on medium-high speed for an additional 15 seconds to ensure the batter is mixed evenly. Add the sugar and vanilla and mix for an additional 20 seconds, or until the mixture is completely smooth. Pour a third of the mixture over the graham cracker crust. Nestle the unfrosted cupcakes into the batter and pour the rest of the cheesecake batter over the cupcakes. The tops and sides of the cupcakes should be completely covered and the pan should be about three-quarters full. Bake for about 50 minutes, until the cheesecake has started to brown on the edges and no longer jiggles when you gently shake the pan. Keep the cheesecake in the pan and allow it to cool completely, then refrigerate it overnight. Before serving, remove the cheesecake from the pan and top with the cherry pie filling.

Oreo Cupcakes with Marshmallow Chocolate Frosting

There are so many different flavors of Oreos in the world, and this recipe will work with any of them. Peanut butter, Double Stuf, Strawberry Milkshake—the choice is yours. Indecisive? I'm a Gemini; I totally understand. Buy a few kinds of cookies and let which flavor is in which cupcake be a complete surprise.

MAKES 22 CUPCAKES

CUPCAKES

¾ cup (1½ sticks) unsalted butter, at room temperature

1½ cups granulated sugar

3 large eggs

2 teaspoons vanilla extract

2 teaspoons baking powder

½ teaspoon baking soda

¼ teaspoon salt

2½ cups unbleached all-purpose flour

1⅓ cups whole milk

22 Oreo cookies, any flavor

FROSTING

4 ounces unsweetened chocolate, broken or chopped into small pieces

2 tablespoons whole milk

1 cup (2 sticks) unsalted butter, at room temperature

1 cup marshmallow creme

2 cups powdered sugar

Oreo cookies, for garnish

1. To make the cupcakes, preheat the oven to 350°F and line 2 standard muffin tins with 22 paper liners. Use a stand mixer fitted with the paddle attachment or a hand mixer on medium speed to combine the butter and sugar for 90 seconds, until fluffy. Add the eggs, one at a time, mixing in each egg completely before adding the next. Use a spatula to scrape down the sides of the bowl. Then, with the mixer on medium-low speed, add the vanilla, baking powder, baking soda, and salt. Turn the mixer up to medium-high speed and mix for another 30 seconds, until all the ingredients are well combined. Finally, add the flour, ½ cup at a time, alternately with the milk, ⅓ cup at a time, mixing until each addition is fully incorporated before adding the next. Scrape down the sides of the bowl again and continue to mix the batter on medium-high speed for 30 seconds, until smooth and creamy.

2. Spoon 2 heaping tablespoons of batter into each cup in the prepared tins. Place a cookie in the center of each cup and gently press it into the batter. Spoon another tablespoon of batter over the top of the cookie so the top and the sides are covered and the cups are about three-quarters full. Bake for 22 to 24 minutes, or until the edges of the cupcakes have started to turn golden brown and the cake springs back when you gently press your finger into the top of it. Allow the cupcakes to rest in the tins for 10 minutes before transferring them to a wire rack to finish cooling.

3. To make the frosting, place the chocolate and milk in a small microwave-safe bowl and microwave on high for 20 seconds. Stir and microwave for another 20 seconds.

Continue to stir the mixture until the chocolate has completely melted and the milk is fully incorporated. Place the bowl in the refrigerator to cool while you prepare the rest of the frosting. Whip the butter and marshmallow creme for about 30 seconds with a stand mixer fitted with the whisk attachment or a hand mixer on medium speed. Add the powdered sugar, ½ cup at a time, whipping on medium-high speed until fluffy. Once the chocolate mixture is cool to the touch, give it another stir and drizzle it into the frosting while whipping on medium-high speed. Continue to mix until combined. Pipe or spread the frosting on top of the cooled cupcakes (see page 137). If you'd like, place some of the leftover cookies in a resealable bag and crush with a rolling pin or wooden spoon. Top the cupcakes with the cookie crumbs.

Cheesecake-Filled Spiced Pumpkin Cupcakes with Nutella Frosting

As with the pumpkin pie–filled cupcakes on page 130, don't assume these cupcakes are only a fall treat because pumpkin is one of the main ingredients—they're just as delicious every other season of the year. They're also versatile! Try pairing the cheesecake center with the chocolate cupcake batter recipe on page 16 or the lime cupcake batter on page 12. Remember that thing I said at the beginning of the book about going rogue? I totally meant it. This recipe would be a great place to start.

MAKES 24 CUPCAKES

CHEESECAKE

1 cup graham cracker crumbs
1 tablespoon light brown sugar, packed
Pinch of salt
3 tablespoons unsalted butter, melted
3 (8-ounce) packages cream cheese, at room temperature
3 eggs
1½ cups granulated sugar
2 tablespoons vanilla extract

CUPCAKES

¾ cup (1½ sticks) unsalted butter, at room temperature
1½ cups granulated sugar
3 large eggs
2 teaspoons vanilla extract
2 teaspoons baking powder
½ teaspoon baking soda
¼ teaspoon salt
1½ cups pumpkin purée (canned is fine)

1 teaspoon ground cloves
1 teaspoon freshly grated nutmeg
1 teaspoon ground cinnamon
1 teaspoon ground allspice
2½ cups unbleached all-purpose flour
1⅓ cups whole milk

FROSTING

1 cup (2 sticks) unsalted butter, at room temperature
½ cup Nutella
2 cups powdered sugar
2 tablespoons whole milk, if needed
Toasted hazelnuts, chopped, for garnish

1. To make the cheesecake, preheat the oven to 325°F and grease a 9-inch square baking pan (or use a nonstick pan). Put the graham cracker crumbs, brown sugar, and salt in a small bowl and mix in the melted butter until the crumbs are moist. Press the crumb mixture evenly

into the bottom of the prepared pan and set aside. To make the cheesecake batter, use a stand mixer fitted with the paddle attachment or a hand mixer on medium speed to whip the cream cheese for 30 seconds, until creamy and smooth. Add the eggs, one at a time, mixing in each egg completely before adding the next. Scrape down the sides of the bowl and whip on medium-high speed for an additional 15 seconds to ensure the batter is mixed evenly. Add the sugar and vanilla and mix for an additional 20 seconds, or until the mixture is completely smooth. Pour the mixture over the graham cracker crust and use a spatula to spread it out evenly over the crust. Bake for about 40 minutes, until the cheesecake has started to brown on the edges and no longer jiggles when you gently shake the pan. Cool the cheesecake completely in the pan. (It's okay to stick it in the refrigerator to speed up the process—I'm impatient, too). Then cut it into 20 bite-sized rectangles.

2. To make the cupcakes, increase the oven temperature to 350°F and line 2 standard muffin tins with 24 paper liners. Use a stand mixer fitted with the paddle attachment or a hand mixer on medium speed to combine the butter and sugar for 90 seconds, until fluffy. Add the eggs, one at a time, mixing in each egg completely before adding the next. Use a spatula to scrape down the sides of the bowl. Then, with the mixer on medium-low speed, add the vanilla, baking powder, baking soda, and salt. Turn the mixer up to medium-high speed and mix for an additional 30 seconds, until all the ingredients are well combined. Then add the pumpkin purée, cloves, nutmeg, cinnamon, and allspice and mix for an additional 20 seconds or so, until just combined. Finally, add the flour, ½ cup at a time, alternately with the milk, ⅓ cup at a time, mixing until each addition is fully incorporated before adding the next. Scrape down the sides of the bowl again and continue to mix the batter on medium-high speed for 30 seconds, until smooth and creamy.

3. Spoon 2 heaping tablespoons of batter into each cup in the prepared tins. Place a piece of cheesecake in the center of each cup and gently press it into the batter. Spoon a small amount of batter over the top of the cheesecake so the top and the sides are covered and the cups are about three-quarters full. Bake for 22 to 24 minutes, until the edges of the cupcakes have started to turn golden brown and the cake springs back when you gently press your finger into the top of it. Allow the cupcakes to rest in the tins for 10 minutes before transferring them to a wire rack to finish cooling.

4. To make the frosting, whip the butter and Nutella for about 30 seconds with a stand mixer fitted with the whisk attachment or a hand mixer on medium speed. Add the powdered sugar, ½ cup at a time, whipping on medium-high speed until fluffy. If the frosting is too thick, add the milk and whip on high for 20 seconds until the frosting is fluffy. Pipe or spread the frosting on top of the cooled cupcakes (see page 137) and, if you'd like, sprinkle with some chopped hazelnuts.

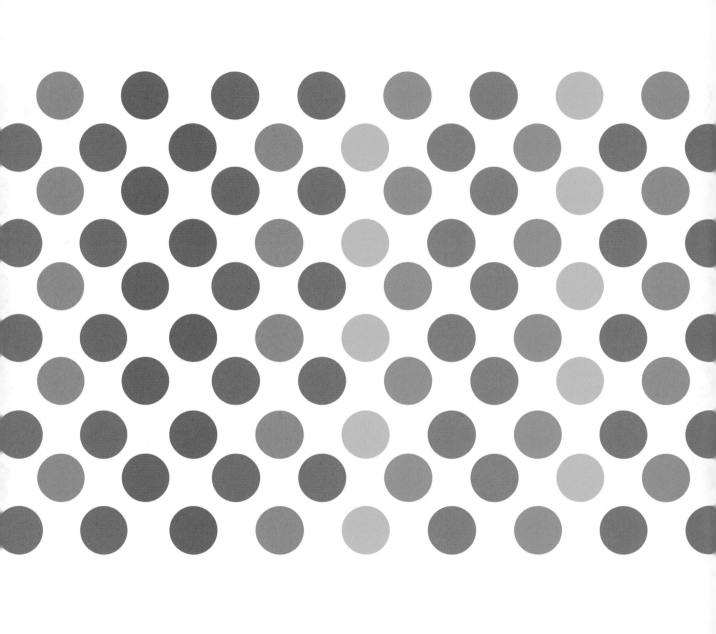

Chapter 2

STRAWBERRIES, PINEAPPLE, FIGS, OH YUM!

One cannot exist on cake alone. A person needs vitamins, minerals, fiber—you know, stuff that isn't butter, salt, and sugar (sigh, I know). But eating a banana or an apple to get a serving of healthy fruit is so . . . obvious. So why not bake it into a cake? Fruit becomes a whole new experience when nestled into the center of a cupcake, and as you can see in this chapter, just about any fruit is fair game in the *Bake It in a Cupcake* world—strawberries, pineapple, even kiwi. And if you don't see your favorites represented here, just mix and match! Try the Apple Crisp Caramel Cupcakes (page 44) with pear. Or the Coconut Kiwi Cupcakes (page 46) with mango. Just look at all the fruit you can cram into a cake! Would it be going too far to call this the health food chapter? Fruit's totally healthy, you know.

Strawberry Shortcake-Filled Chocolate Cupcakes with Strawberry Cream Cheese Frosting

I didn't think it could be done, either. Bake a miniature strawberry shortcake into a cupcake? Clearly that's where the line is drawn, right? Nope. It's totally possible, and it tastes amazing. I love these topped with a pile of strawberry cream cheese frosting, but they'd be just as good with some fresh, lightly sweetened whipped cream.

MAKES 20 CUPCAKES

SHORTCAKES

1 pint fresh strawberries

2 tablespoons sugar

1 (14-ounce) package scone mix, made as directed on the box

CUPCAKES

4 ounces unsweetened chocolate, broken or chopped into small pieces

1⅓ cups plus 2 tablespoons whole milk

¾ cup (1½ sticks) unsalted butter, at room temperature

1½ cups granulated sugar

3 large eggs

2 teaspoons vanilla extract

2 teaspoons baking powder

½ teaspoon baking soda

¼ teaspoon salt

½ cup unsweetened cocoa powder

2½ cups unbleached all-purpose flour

FROSTING

1 pint fresh strawberries

1 cup (2 sticks) unsalted butter, at room temperature

8 ounces cream cheese, at room temperature

2 cups powdered sugar

1. To make the shortcakes, preheat the oven to 425°F and line a cookie sheet with parchment paper. Remove the stems and leaves from the strawberries and cut the berries into very small chunks. Place them in a medium bowl with the sugar and stir until well coated. Set them aside. Knead the prepared scone dough 5 or 6 times, folding it over onto itself, and then roll it out until about 1 inch thick on a generously floured smooth surface. Use a 2-inch round cookie cutter to cut out 20 disks of dough. Place them on the prepared cookie sheet and bake for 8 to 10 minutes, until the scones have puffed up and started to turn golden brown.

continued on page 43 ➡

Allow them to cool on the cookie sheet while you make the cupcake batter.

2. To make the cupcakes, turn the oven down to 350°F. Line 2 standard muffin tins with 20 paper liners. Place the chocolate and 2 tablespoons of the milk in a small microwave-safe bowl and microwave for 20 seconds on high. Stir and microwave for another 20 seconds. Stir the mixture until the chocolate has completely melted and the cream is fully incorporated. Place the bowl in the refrigerator so it can cool while you prepare the rest of the cupcake batter.

3. Use a stand mixer fitted with the paddle attachment or a hand mixer on medium speed to combine the butter and sugar for 90 seconds, until fluffy. Add the eggs, one at a time, mixing in each egg completely before adding the next. Use a spatula to scrape down the sides of the bowl. Then, with the mixer on medium-low speed, add the vanilla, baking powder, baking soda, and salt. Add the cocoa powder. Turn the mixer up to medium-high speed and mix for an additional 30 seconds, until all the ingredients are well combined. Scrape down the sides of the bowl. Add the flour, ½ cup at a time, alternately with the remaining 1⅓ cups milk, ⅓ cup at a time, mixing until each addition is fully incorporated before adding the next. Finally, with the mixer on medium-high, drizzle in the cooled chocolate mixture. Continue to mix the batter on medium-high speed for 30 seconds, until smooth and creamy.

4. Cut all the scones in half horizontally to make a top and a bottom. Spoon a heaping tablespoon of batter into each cup in the prepared tins. Place the bottom of the shortcake in the batter and press it down gently. Top that with a teaspoon of the chopped strawberries and top them with the other piece of shortcake. Cover the shortcake with another heaping tablespoon of batter so the top and sides are completely covered and the cup is about three-quarters full. Bake at 350°F for about 25 minutes, until the edges and tops of the cupcakes have set and the cake springs back when you gently press your finger into the top of it. Allow the cupcakes to cool in the tins for at least 10 minutes before moving to a wire rack to cool completely.

5. To make the frosting, remove the leaves and stems from the strawberries and purée the berries in a blender or food processor. Set the purée aside. Whip the butter and cream cheese together for about 30 seconds with a stand mixer fitted with the whisk attachment or a hand mixer on medium speed. Add the powdered sugar, ½ cup at a time, whipping on medium-high speed until fluffy. Pour in half of the strawberry purée and whip for another 30 seconds on medium-high speed. Give it a taste and, if you'd like, add more of the strawberry purée. If the frosting begins to get too runny, add some more powdered sugar until you get the desired consistency. Pipe or spread the frosting on top of the cooled cupcakes (see page 137).

Apple Crisp Caramel Cupcakes with Ice Cream

I dare you to find a more delicious way to use apples than with apple crisp. It just can't be done. Apple pie is good, yeah, and apple cake is nice, too. Apple tarts, apple cookies, baked apples with maple syrup—they're all great. But as far as I am concerned, apple crisp rules them all. The crunchy oat topping; the spices; the gooey, soft apples caramelized with butter and brown sugar . . . sheer perfection. So of course I took that perfection and put it into a cupcake. And while this recipe is great with some salted caramel frosting (page 86) or a basic vanilla buttercream (page 16), after much research, I found the best topping was a generous scoop of vanilla ice cream placed on top of the warm cupcake.

MAKES 24 CUPCAKES

APPLE CRISP TOPPING
¾ cup rolled oats
½ cup walnuts, chopped
½ cup (1 stick) unsalted butter, at room temperature
2 tablespoons unbleached all-purpose flour
2 tablespoons light brown sugar
2 teaspoons ground cinnamon
Pinch of salt

APPLE FILLING
2 medium apples, any variety (I prefer Granny Smith or something equally tart)
1 tablespoon lemon juice (fresh or bottled)
2 tablespoons unsalted butter
2 tablespoons granulated sugar
2 tablespoons light brown sugar
2 teaspoons ground cinnamon
¼ teaspoon salt

CUPCAKES
¾ cup (1½ sticks) unsalted butter, at room temperature
1¼ cups granulated sugar
3 large eggs
2 teaspoons vanilla extract
2 teaspoons baking powder
½ teaspoon baking soda
½ teaspoon salt
2½ cups unbleached all-purpose flour
1 cup whole milk

1. To make the apple crisp topping, place all the ingredients in a small bowl and use your hands or a fork to mix the ingredients together until evenly combined and crumbly.

2. To make the apple filling, peel, core, and chop the apples into ¼-inch pieces. Place them in a bowl, add the lemon juice, and stir until the apples are coated. Set aside. Place the butter, granulated sugar, brown sugar, cinnamon, and salt in a skillet and cook over medium-high heat, stirring every couple of minutes, until the butter is melted and the sugar has dissolved. Once the mixture is bubbling, add the apples and stir so they're coated evenly. Lower the heat to medium and allow the mixture to cook for about 5 minutes, until the apples have begun to soften (they'll cook more in the oven, so it's okay if they're al dente).

3. To make the cupcakes, preheat the oven to 350°F and line 2 standard muffin tins with 24 paper liners. Use a stand mixer fitted with the paddle attachment or a hand mixer on medium speed to combine the butter and sugar for 90 seconds, until fluffy. Add the eggs, one at a time, mixing in each egg completely before adding the next. Use a spatula to scrape down the sides of the bowl. Then, with the mixer on medium-low speed, add the vanilla, baking powder, baking soda, and salt. Turn the mixer up to medium-high speed and mix for an additional 30 seconds, until all the ingredients are well combined. Finally, add the flour, ½ cup at a time, alternately with the milk, ⅓ cup at a time, mixing until each addition is fully incorporated before adding the next. Scrape down the sides of the bowl again and continue to mix the batter on medium-high speed for 30 seconds, until smooth and creamy.

4. Spoon 2 heaping tablespoons of batter into each cup in the prepared tins so they're two-thirds full. Spoon a heaping teaspoon of the apple mixture (okay, maybe a tiny bit more) over the batter and sprinkle about a teaspoon of the crumbly topping over that. Bake for about 25 minutes, or until the edges of the cupcakes have started to turn golden brown and the cake around the sides of the apple mixture is set (it'll bounce back when you gently press your finger into it). Allow the cupcakes to rest in the tins for 10 minutes before transferring them to a wire rack to cool a bit. Serve warm with a scoop of vanilla ice cream.

Coconut Kiwi Cupcakes with Pineapple Frosting

Take just one bite of these cupcakes and you will shout, "Where am I, and when did I get transported to this tropical island?" thanks to the triple threat of flavors like kiwi, coconut, and pineapple. Not a kiwi fan? That's okay! Substitute chopped mango, papaya, or even banana. (And it probably wouldn't be a bad idea to wear sunscreen while baking, just in case.)

MAKES 18 CUPCAKES

CUPCAKES

1 cup finely shredded unsweetened coconut, plus more for garnish

5 large kiwis

3/4 cup (1 1/2 sticks) unsalted butter, at room temperature

1 1/2 cups granulated sugar

3 large eggs

2 teaspoons vanilla extract

2 teaspoons baking powder

1/2 teaspoon baking soda

1/4 teaspoon salt

3/4 cup cream of coconut

2 1/2 cups unbleached all-purpose flour

1 1/3 cups whole milk

FROSTING

1 cup (2 sticks) unsalted butter, at room temperature

2 cups powdered sugar, or more as needed

1 (8-ounce) can crushed pineapple, drained

2 tablespoons whole milk, if needed

1. Begin by toasting the coconut. Preheat the oven to 350°F. Spread the coconut out in a thin layer on a cookie sheet that has been lined with parchment paper and place the cookie sheet in the oven for about 10 minutes, until the coconut has started to turn golden brown. Remove from the oven and allow to cool while you make the cupcakes.

2. To make the cupcakes, leave the oven at 350°F and line 2 standard muffin tins with 18 paper liners. Peel and slice the kiwis 1/4 inch thick, discarding the ends so you have slices that will give you a bite of kiwi in each bite of cupcake. Lay the slices out on a paper towel and top with another paper towel to absorb some moisture while you mix the cupcake batter. Use a stand mixer fitted with the paddle attachment or a hand mixer on medium speed to combine the butter and sugar for 90 seconds, until fluffy. Add the eggs, one at a time, mixing in each egg completely before adding the next. With the mixer on medium-low speed, add the vanilla,

baking powder, baking soda, and salt. Turn the mixer up to medium-high speed and mix for an additional 30 seconds, until all the ingredients are well combined. Add the cream of coconut and toasted coconut and mix on medium-high for an additional 20 seconds or so, until combined. Finally, add the flour, ½ cup at a time, alternately with the milk, ⅓ cup at a time, mixing until each addition is fully incorporated before adding the next. Continue to mix the batter on medium-high speed for 30 seconds, until smooth and creamy.

3. Pour the batter into each cup in the prepared tins so they are about three-quarters full. Place a slice of kiwi in each cup and gently press it into the batter. Bake for about 25 minutes, until the edges of the cupcakes have turned golden brown and the cake springs back when you gently press your finger into the top of it.

Allow the cupcakes to cool in the tins for at least 10 minutes before moving them to a wire rack to cool completely.

4. To make the frosting, whip the butter for about 30 seconds with a stand mixer fitted with the whisk attachment or a hand mixer on medium speed. Add the powdered sugar, ½ cup at a time, whipping on medium-high speed until fluffy. With the mixer on medium speed, add the pineapple a heaping spoonful at a time. The acid in the pineapple juice might cause the frosting to separate a little—if this happens, just add more powdered sugar, a couple spoonfuls at a time, until the consistency is smooth again. If the frosting becomes too thick, add the milk. Pipe or spread the frosting on top of the cooled cupcakes (see page 137) and top them with some toasted coconut.

Mission Fig Spiced Cupcakes with Vanilla Frosting

Figs are a wonderful and versatile ingredient to cook and bake with—they can be used in both sweet and savory dishes, and for this particular recipe you can use either fresh or dried figs. Keep in mind, if using fresh figs, you may need to add a couple minutes to the baking time, since the fruit will release some moisture as it bakes.

MAKES 18 CUPCAKES

CUPCAKES

1 cup (2 sticks) unsalted butter, at room
   temperature
1½ cups granulated sugar
3 large eggs
2 teaspoons vanilla extract
2 teaspoons baking powder
½ teaspoon baking soda
¼ teaspoon salt
2 teaspoons ground cinnamon
1 teaspoon freshly grated nutmeg
1 teaspoon ground cloves
2½ cups unbleached all-purpose flour
1 cup low-fat buttermilk
18 fresh or 18 to 36 dried Mission figs, stemmed

FROSTING

1 cup (2 sticks) unsalted butter, at room
   temperature
2 cups powdered sugar
2 teaspoons vanilla extract
2 tablespoons whole milk, if needed
Ground cinnamon, for garnish

1. To make the cupcakes, preheat the oven to 350°F and line 2 standard muffin tins with 18 paper liners. Use a stand mixer fitted with the paddle attachment or a hand mixer on medium speed to combine the butter and sugar for 90 seconds, until fluffy. Add the eggs, one at a time, mixing in each egg completely before adding the next. Use a spatula to scrape down the sides of the bowl. Then, with the mixer on medium-low speed, add the vanilla, baking powder, baking soda, and salt. Turn the mixer up to medium-high speed and mix for an additional 30 seconds, until all the ingredients are well combined. Then add the cinnamon,

continued on page 50 ⇒

nutmeg, and cloves and mix for an additional 20 seconds or so, until just combined. Finally, add the flour, ½ cup at a time, alternately with the buttermilk, ⅓ cup at a time, mixing until each addition is fully incorporated before adding the next. Scrape down the sides of the bowl again and continue to mix the batter on medium-high speed for 30 seconds, until smooth and creamy.

2. Spoon 2 heaping tablespoons of batter into each cup in the prepared tins. Place a fig in the center of each cup and gently press it into the batter. (If you are using dried figs, which are smaller than fresh ones, you might want to put 2 pieces of fruit in each cup—it's up to you.) Spoon a small amount of batter over the top of the fig so the top and the sides of the fruit are covered and the tins are about three-quarters full. Bake for 22 to 24 minutes, or until the edges of the cupcakes have started to turn golden brown and the cake springs back when you gently press your finger into the top of it. Allow the cupcakes to rest in the tins for 10 minutes before transferring them to a wire rack to finish cooling.

3. To make the frosting, whip the butter for about 30 seconds with a stand mixer fitted with the whisk attachment or a hand mixer on medium speed. Add the powdered sugar, ½ cup at a time, whipping on medium-high speed until fluffy. Add the vanilla and whip until just combined. If the frosting is too thick, add the milk and whip on high for 20 seconds, until the frosting is fluffy. Pipe or spread the frosting on top of the cooled cupcakes (see page 137) and, if you'd like, sprinkle with some cinnamon.

Upside-Down Meyer Lemon Brownie Cupcakes

These brownies were the result of a happy accident. I initially wanted to make an upside-down lemon cupcake, but I didn't have enough milk to make cupcake batter and I was too lazy to go to the store. So I tried my idea with brownies, instead, and hoped for the best. The end result is a very decadent dessert that should be eaten with a fork (they're quite sticky), making them the perfect choice for those occasions when you need something a little fancier than your average cupcake. And they look especially pretty when plated with some fresh, lightly sweetened whipped cream and chocolate shavings.

When making these brownie cupcakes, you must use Meyer lemons, which are less tart than other lemons and have an edible peel.

MAKES 12 BROWNIE CUPCAKES

BROWNIES

¾ cup (2 sticks) plus 4 tablespoons (½ stick) unsalted butter

2 cups plus 2 tablespoons plus 2 tablespoons granulated sugar

2 tablespoons dark muscovado sugar

2 large Meyer lemons

4 ounces unsweetened chocolate, broken or chopped into small pieces

3 large eggs

½ teaspoon salt

1 teaspoon plus 1 teaspoon vanilla extract

1 cup unbleached all-purpose flour

1 cup heavy whipping cream

Chocolate shavings or cacao nibs, for garnish

1. To make the brownies, preheat the oven to 350°F and grease a 12-cup standard muffin tin. Place 4 tablespoons (½ stick) of the butter, 2 tablespoons of the granulated sugar, and the muscovado sugar in a medium saucepan and bring to a boil over medium heat, stirring occasionally. Cook for 8 to 10 minutes, until all the sugar has dissolved and the mixture has started to thicken (it should coat the back of the spoon). Put 1 teaspoon of the caramel mixture into the bottom of each greased muffin cup.

2. Thoroughly wash the Meyer lemons and, using a very sharp knife or a mandoline, slice them (with their peel still on) into 12 very thin (⅛-inch) slices. Remove any seeds, blot the lemon slices dry on a paper towel, and place a slice in each muffin cup. (If the slices are too wide to fit into the bottom of the cup, you can cut out a

continued on page 53 ⇒

small section of the lemon and the peel to help them fit better.) Set aside.

3. Place the chocolate and the remaining ¾ cup butter (1 ½ sticks) in a medium microwave-safe bowl and microwave on high for 90 seconds, stopping halfway through to stir the butter and chocolate together. After 90 seconds, continue to stir the butter and chocolate until all the chocolate chunks have completely melted into the butter. (If you microwave any longer, you risk burning the chocolate, so it's best to be patient and let the chocolate melt slowly while you stir.) Using a wooden spoon, stir in 2 cups of the remaining granulated sugar. It will be thick and grainy, and the sugar should be distributed evenly. Next, stir in the eggs one at a time, mixing in each one completely before adding the next, until the mixture is smooth. Add the salt and 1 teaspoon of the vanilla and stir for an additional 20 seconds, until they're both incorporated. Finally, mix in the flour until just combined, taking care not to overstir.

4. Spoon the brownie batter over the lemon slices, filling the cups three-quarters full. Bake for 23 minutes, until the brownies have set. The caramel mixture and juice from the lemons might bubble up around the edges, so you may want to set your tin on a larger sheet cake pan to catch any drips. When the brownies are done (a toothpick inserted into the center of a brownie should come out clean), remove them from the oven and allow them to cool in the tin for 15 minutes. While they're still warm, gently run a knife around the sides of the brownies to loosen them from the cups. Place a larger sheet cake or cookie pan over the top of the muffin tin and invert the brownies.

5. Before serving, use a stand mixer with the whisk attachment or a hand mixer to whip the cream, remaining 2 tablespoons granulated sugar, and remaining 1 teaspoon vanilla until stiff peaks form. Serve each brownie with a spoonful of fresh whipped cream and a few chocolate shavings.

Inside-Out Pineapple Upside-Down Cupcakes

I love pineapple, so of course I love pineapple upside-down cake. This cupcake is an ode to the classic in which I have turned the cake not only right side up but also inside out, with the caramelized pineapple inside and the maraschino cherry on top. It's just as delicious as any pineapple upside-down cake you've ever had, yet more portable. Which is good, since all your friends will constantly be asking for you to bring these cupcakes to their parties after just one taste.

MAKES 20 CUPCAKES

PINEAPPLE FILLING
2 tablespoons unsalted butter
3 tablespoons brown sugar
2 (8-ounce) cans crushed pineapple, drained
1/4 teaspoon salt

CUPCAKES
3/4 cup (1 1/2 sticks) unsalted butter, at room
   temperature
1 1/2 cups granulated sugar
3 large eggs
2 teaspoons vanilla extract
2 teaspoons baking powder
1/2 teaspoon baking soda
1/4 teaspoon salt
2 1/2 cups unbleached all-purpose flour
1 1/3 cups whole milk

FROSTING
1 cup (2 sticks) unsalted butter, at room
   temperature
2 cups powdered sugar
1 (10-ounce) jar maraschino cherries (with
   stems, if possible)

1. To make the pineapple filling, melt the butter and brown sugar together in a medium saucepan over medium heat. Once all the sugar is dissolved, add the pineapple and stir so all the fruit is incorporated into the sugar mixture. Stir in the salt and cook over medium heat for about 10 minutes, stirring every couple of minutes, until the pineapple mixture has thickened and all the excess pineapple juice has evaporated. Remove from the heat and set aside to cool while you make the cupcakes.

2. To make the cupcakes, preheat the oven to 350°F and line 2 standard muffin tins with 20 paper liners. Use a stand mixer fitted with the paddle attachment or a hand mixer on medium speed to combine the butter and sugar for 90 seconds, until fluffy. Add the eggs, one at a time, mixing in each egg completely before adding the next. With the mixer on medium-low speed, add the vanilla, baking powder, baking soda, and salt. Turn the mixer up to medium-high speed and mix for an additional 30 seconds, until all the ingredients are well combined. Finally, add the flour, ½ cup at a time, alternately with the milk, ⅓ cup at a time, mixing until each addition is fully incorporated before adding the next. Continue to mix the batter on medium-high speed for 30 seconds, until smooth and creamy.

3. Spoon a heaping tablespoon of batter into each cup in the prepared tins. Spoon a heaping tea-spoon of the cooled pineapple mixture into the center of the batter and cover the mixture with another heaping tablespoon of batter so the cup is about three-quarters full. Bake for about 24 minutes, until the edges and tops of the cupcakes have turned golden brown and the cake springs back when you gently press your finger into the top of it. Allow the cupcakes to cool in the tin for at least 10 minutes before moving them to a wire rack to cool completely.

4. To make the frosting, begin by whipping the butter for about 30 seconds with a stand mixer fitted with the whisk attachment or a hand mixer on medium speed. Add the powdered sugar, ½ cup at a time, whipping on medium-high speed until fluffy. With the mixer on medium speed, slowly drizzle in the liquid from the jar of maraschino cherries. You'll use half to three-quarters of the liquid (more or less, to taste). Pipe or spread the frosting on top of the cooled cupcakes (see page 137) and top each cupcake with a cherry.

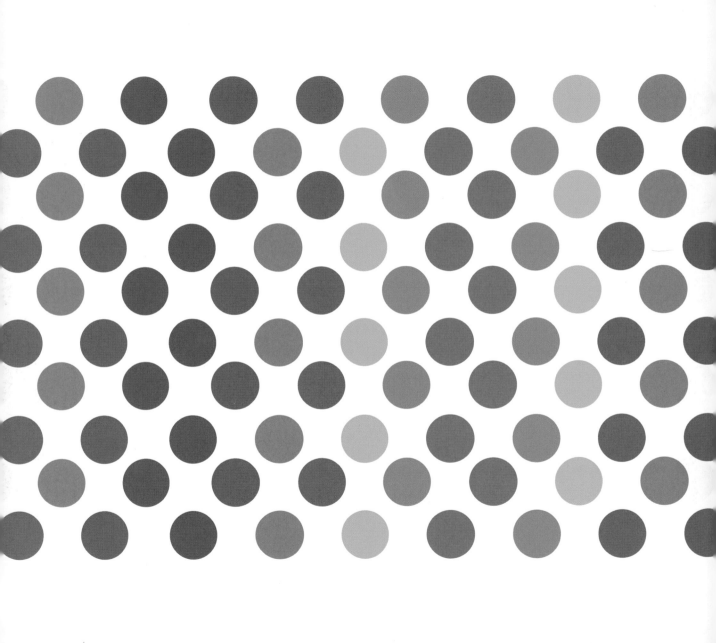

BREAKFAST OF CHAMPIONS

Cereal schmereal, the new way to start the day comes in a cake. Okay, so maybe a butter-filled sugar bomb isn't the best morning snack, but seeing as how breakfast is my favorite meal (well, second favorite if you count dessert as a meal, which I do), I just had to find creative ways to bake breakfast into a cake. As you can see, I totally succeeded. Now all your breakfast favorites are tucked into the center of a cupcake—pancakes, waffles, oatmeal, cinnamon rolls. Even cereal and milk!

If you'd rather not start your day with something sweet, be sure to check out Chapter 6, the savory chapter, where you'll find a few more options appropriate for breakfast, like the Egg-Filled Croissant Cups with Swiss Cheese and Chives (page 99).

There's no need to thank me. I was happy to do it.

Blueberry Pancake Cupcakes with Maple Syrup

You can totally have cupcakes for breakfast when breakfast is in the cupcake. To make the pancakes, you should use your favorite pancake batter, be it boxed or homemade. You'll need at least 2 cups to get enough silver-dollar pancakes for the cupcakes. While this recipe uses blueberries, you could also try making the pancakes with raspberries or chocolate chips.

MAKES 20 CUPCAKES

PANCAKES
2 cups pancake batter, made as directed on the box
1 cup fresh blueberries

CUPCAKES
¾ cup (1½ sticks) unsalted butter, at room temperature
1½ cups granulated sugar
3 large eggs
2 teaspoons vanilla extract
2 teaspoons baking powder
½ teaspoon baking soda
¼ teaspoon salt
2½ cups unbleached all-purpose flour
1⅓ cups whole milk
Maple syrup, for serving

1. To make the pancakes, heat a skillet or a nonstick frying pan over medium-high heat. When it's hot, drop heaping tablespoons of the prepared pancake batter onto the pan, making 20 small (2-inch) pancakes. While the pancake batter begins to set around the edges, drop 3 or 4 blueberries into each pancake. Once bubbles have formed in the pancake batter and the bottom of the pancakes are golden brown (it will take only a few minutes), flip the pancakes over and continue to cook them until the other side is also golden brown. Remove the pancakes from the heat and set aside.

2. To make the cupcakes, preheat the oven to 350°F and line 2 standard muffin tins with 20 paper liners. Use a stand mixer fitted with the paddle attachment or a hand mixer on medium speed to combine the butter and sugar for 90 seconds, until fluffy. Add the eggs, one at a time, mixing in each egg completely before adding the next. Use a spatula to scrape down the sides of the bowl. Then, with the mixer on medium-low speed, add the vanilla, baking

continued on page 61 ➡

powder, baking soda, and salt. Turn the mixer up to medium-high speed and mix for an additional 30 seconds, so all the ingredients are well combined. Finally, add the flour, ½ cup at a time, alternately with the milk, ⅓ cup at a time, mixing until each addition is fully incorporated before adding the next. Scrape down the sides of the bowl again and continue to mix the batter on medium-high speed for 30 seconds, until smooth and creamy.

3. Pour the batter into each cup in the prepared tins so they're about half full. Place a pancake in the center of the cup and press it gently into the batter. (You could also put the pancake inside the cupcake—put a heaping tablespoon of batter into the cup, then the pancake, then another tablespoon of batter—but I like to leave the pancake on the top because it looks cuter that way.) Bake for about 25 minutes, until the cupcakes have turned golden brown and they spring back when you gently press your finger into the top of the pancake. Allow the cupcakes to cool in the tins for at least 10 minutes before moving them to a wire rack to cool. Right before serving the cupcakes, drizzle them with some maple syrup (or whatever it is you like to put on top of your pancakes).

Cinnamon Roll Vanilla Cupcakes with Vanilla Bean Glaze

Could you make these cupcakes using homemade cinnamon rolls? Sure. But that's a lot of kneading and rising and waiting and cutting, and why do all that when you're ready to make cupcakes *now*? So I used some packaged cinnamon roll dough to save time (and effort), and it worked wonderfully. You'll never want to eat a cakeless cinnamon roll again.

MAKES 24 CUPCAKES

CUPCAKES
1 (17-ounce) tube refrigerated cinnamon rolls (not the "grand" size)
¾ cup (1½ sticks) unsalted butter, at room temperature
1½ cups granulated sugar
3 large eggs
2 teaspoons vanilla extract
2 teaspoons baking powder
½ teaspoon baking soda
¼ teaspoon salt
2½ cups unbleached all-purpose flour
1⅓ cups whole milk

VANILLA BEAN GLAZE
1 cup powdered sugar, or more as needed
2 tablespoons milk, or more as needed
Seeds from ½ vanilla bean (see page 63)

1. To make the cupcakes, preheat the oven to 350°F. Lightly grease a 24-cup miniature muffin tin. Open the tube of cinnamon roll dough and separate the cinnamon rolls onto a cutting board. Cut each roll into 3 equal parts so you have 24 pieces. Roll each piece of dough into a ball and place a ball in each prepared cup. Bake for about 10 minutes, until the cinnamon rolls have risen and turned golden brown. Set them aside to cool in the tin while you make the cupcake batter.

2. Line 2 standard muffin tins with 24 paper liners. Use a stand mixer fitted with the paddle attachment or a hand mixer on medium speed to combine the butter and sugar for 90 seconds, until fluffy. Add the eggs, one at a time, mixing in each egg completely before adding the next. Use a spatula to scrape down the sides of the bowl. Then, with the mixer on medium-low speed, add the vanilla, baking powder, baking soda, and salt. Turn the mixer

up to medium-high speed and mix for an additional 30 seconds, until all the ingredients are well combined. Finally, add the flour, ½ cup at a time, alternately with the milk, ⅓ cup at a time, mixing until each addition is fully incorporated before adding the next. Scrape down the sides of the bowl again and continue to mix the batter on medium-high speed for 30 seconds, until smooth and creamy.

3. Spoon a heaping tablespoon of batter into each cup in the prepared tins. Place a cooled cinnamon roll into the center of the batter and press it gently. You don't want the roll to touch the bottom of the tin. Cover the rolls with another heaping tablespoon of batter so the top and sides of the roll are completely covered and the cup is about three-quarters full. (If your cinnamon rolls rose a lot, it's okay if the tops stick up out of the batter a little bit.) Bake for 25 minutes, until the edges and tops of the cupcakes have turned golden brown and the cake springs back when you gently press your finger into the top of it. Allow the cupcakes to cool in the tins for at least 10 minutes while you prepare the glaze.

4. To make the glaze, place the powdered sugar in a small bowl. While whisking the sugar, drizzle in the milk. Continue to whisk until all the milk has been incorporated into the sugar. If your glaze is too thick, add a little more milk until you've reached the desired consistency. You want to be able to pour it, but it shouldn't be so runny that it runs right off the cupcakes. If it's too runny, add more powdered sugar. Finally, stir in the vanilla seeds. Pour the glaze over the cupcakes while they're still warm.

BAKER'S TIP

Don't know how to use vanilla bean? It's easy. The vanilla bean has a wonderful, clean vanilla flavor, and it can replace vanilla extract in almost any cake recipe. To get the seeds from the vanilla bean, use a sharp knife to cut the bean in half lengthwise. Scrape the blade of the knife along both sides of the inside of the bean, scooping out all the seeds. The black seeds are very small, and they'll stick together. Use a spatula or spoon to scrape the seeds off the knife, then mix them into your batter.

French Toast Cheesecake Cupcakes

In this recipe, thick slices of spiced, eggy French toast are baked into rich, creamy cheesecake cupcakes and finished off with a drizzle of maple syrup. Finally a cheesecake that could double as breakfast. I'm not the only person who's always wished for that, right?

MAKES 24 CUPCAKES

FRENCH TOAST
1 loaf brioche
2 cups whole milk
4 large eggs
1 tablespoon vanilla extract
1 tablespoon ground cinnamon
½ teaspoon freshly grated nutmeg

CHEESECAKE
1½ cups graham cracker crumbs
4 tablespoons (½ stick) butter, melted
1 teaspoon ground cinnamon
3 (8-ounce) packages cream cheese
1 cup granulated sugar
3 large eggs
2 teaspoons vanilla extract
Maple syrup or fresh strawberries, for serving

1. To make the French toast, cut the bread into 1-inch-thick slices. In a medium bowl, whisk together the milk, eggs, vanilla, cinnamon, and nutmeg, then pour the mixture into a large casserole dish. Preheat a nonstick electric griddle to 350° F or heat a stovetop griddle or large frying pan over medium-high heat. While it heats, press the slices of bread into the egg mixture and let them soak for at least 5 minutes, flipping them over a couple times so the bread is soaked all the way through. Place the slices on the heated griddle and cook each side for about 5 minutes. The bread will turn a nice, deep golden brown color, and it shouldn't feel soggy when you lightly press your finger or the corner of your spatula against the surface of it. Put the French toast on a plate and set aside.

2. To make the cheesecake, in a small bowl, use a spoon to mix together the graham cracker crumbs, melted butter, and cinnamon until all the crumbs have been coated evenly with the butter. The mixture will be moist, but it should not be mushy. Gently and evenly press the mixture into the bottom of 24 cups in 2 standard muffin tins.

3. To make the cheesecake filling, use a stand mixer fitted with the paddle attachment or a hand mixer on medium-high speed to whip the cream cheese and sugar together for 30 seconds. Then add the eggs, one at a time, and the vanilla and mix for 30 more seconds

on medium-high speed. The mixture will be very thick and smooth.

4. Scoop a heaping tablespoon of cheesecake filling into the cups and gently spread it out over the graham cracker crust. Cut the French toast into 24 bite-sized pieces and place a piece in each cup, on top of the cheesecake filling. Gently press it into the filling, taking care not to press it all the way to the bottom. Spread another heaping tablespoon of cheesecake filling over the toast, making sure all the bread is covered, so the cups are no more than three-quarters full—the cheesecake will rise a bit as it bakes. Give the pan a light shake to help the filling settle down around the toast.

5. Bake the cupcakes for about 30 minutes, until they have puffed up and started to brown on top. It's fine if the cheesecake still jiggles a tiny bit when you lightly shake the pan; it will set as it cools.

6. Allow the cheesecakes to cool for at least 30 minutes, then refrigerate for at least 2 hours. To remove the cheesecakes, use a knife to circle around the edges of the cups and then gently lift them out with a fork. Serve each cupcake with a drizzle of maple syrup or even a sliced strawberry or two. It *is* French toast, after all!

Breakfast Cereal Cupcakes with Malted-Milk Frosting

Who needs a bowl and spoon to enjoy cereal when you can have it delivered straight to your mouth by way of a delicious cupcake? Personally, when making these cupcakes, I think Fruity Pebbles are the way to go, but feel free to experiment with your favorites for a variety of textures and flavors. The list of possibilities is literally endless . . . or at least as long as the cereal aisle.

MAKES 24 CUPCAKES

CUPCAKES
¾ cup (1½ sticks) unsalted butter, at room temperature

1½ cups granulated sugar

3 large eggs

2 teaspoons vanilla extract

2 teaspoons baking powder

½ teaspoon baking soda

¼ teaspoon salt

2 ripe bananas, mashed

2½ cups unbleached all-purpose flour

1⅓ cups whole milk

2 cups Fruity Pebbles (or another favorite) cereal, plus more for garnish

FROSTING
1 cup (2 sticks) unsalted butter, at room temperature

2 cups powdered sugar

2 tablespoons malted milk powder

2 tablespoons whole milk, if needed

1. To make the cupcakes, preheat the oven to 350°F and line 2 standard muffin tins with 24 paper liners. Use a stand mixer fitted with the paddle attachment or a hand mixer on medium speed to combine the butter and sugar for 90 seconds, until fluffy. Add the eggs, one at a time, mixing in each egg completely before adding the next. Use a spatula to scrape down the sides of the bowl. Then, with the mixer on medium-low speed, add the vanilla, baking powder, baking soda, and salt. Turn the mixer up to medium-high speed and mix until all the ingredients are well combined. Add the mashed banana and mix for an additional 20 seconds or so. Finally, add the flour, ½ cup at a time, alternately with the milk, ⅓ cup at a time, mixing until each addition is fully incorporated before adding the next. Scrape down the sides of the bowl again and continue to mix the batter on medium-high speed an additional 30 seconds, until smooth and creamy.

continued on page 68 ➡

Using a wooden spoon or spatula, stir in the cereal until just combined.

2. Pour the batter into the cups so they are about three-quarters full. Bake for 24 minutes, or until the edges of the cupcakes have started to turn golden brown and the cake springs back when you gently press your finger into the top of it. Allow the cupcakes to rest in the tins for 10 minutes before transferring them to a wire rack to finish cooling.

3. To make the frosting, whip the butter for about 30 seconds with a stand mixer fitted with the whisk attachment or a hand mixer on medium speed. Add the powdered sugar, ½ cup at a time, whipping on medium-high speed until fluffy. Add the malted milk powder and whip until just combined. If the frosting is too thick, add the milk and whip on high for 20 seconds, until the frosting is fluffy. Pipe or spread the frosting on top of the cooled cupcakes (see page 137) and decorate with some extra cereal.

Waffle Cupcakes with Strawberries and Whipped Cream

Much like the Blueberry Pancake Cupcakes (page 59), these cupcakes work best when the waffles are on the top, as opposed to inside, only because then you can top them as you would any other waffles and they look extra cute. I prefer mine with strawberries and whipped cream, but you can use whatever you like—syrup, chocolate chips, bananas, blueberries. I also use frozen waffles as a shortcut. Can you use homemade waffles? Of course. But I recommend not using a Belgian-style waffle maker, as the waffles are too thick and the squares are too big.

MAKES 24 CUPCAKES

CUPCAKES

¾ cup (1½ sticks) unsalted butter, at room temperature
1½ cups granulated sugar
3 large eggs
2 teaspoons vanilla extract
2 teaspoons baking powder
½ teaspoon baking soda
¼ teaspoon salt
2½ cups unbleached all-purpose flour
1⅓ cups whole milk
5 frozen waffles, cut into quarters

WHIPPED CREAM

1 cup heavy whipping cream
2 tablespoons granulated sugar
1 teaspoon vanilla extract
1 cup sliced strawberries

1. To make the cupcakes, preheat the oven to 350°F and line 2 standard muffin tins with 24 paper liners. Use a stand mixer fitted with the paddle attachment or a hand mixer on medium speed to combine the butter and sugar for 90 seconds, until fluffy. Add the eggs, one at a time, mixing in each egg completely before adding the next. Use a spatula to scrape down the sides of the bowl. Then, with the mixer on medium-low speed, add the vanilla, baking powder, baking soda, and salt. Turn the mixer up to medium-high speed and mix until all the ingredients are well combined. Finally, add the flour, ½ cup at a time, alternately with the milk, ⅓ cup at a time, mixing until each addition is fully incorporated before adding the next. Scrape down the sides of the bowl again and continue to mix the batter on medium-high speed for 30 seconds, until smooth and creamy.

continued on page 70 ➡

2. Pour the batter into the prepared cups so they are about two-thirds full. Place a waffle piece in the center of each cup and press it gently into the batter. (You could also put the waffle inside the cupcake—put a heaping tablespoon of batter into the cup, then the waffle, then another tablespoon of batter—but I like to leave the waffle on the top because it looks cuter that way.) Bake for 25 minutes, or until the edges of the cupcakes have started to turn golden brown and the cake springs back when you gently press your finger into the top of it. Allow the cupcakes to rest in the tins for 10 minutes before transferring them to a wire rack to finish cooling.

3. Before serving, use a stand mixer fitted with the whisk attachment or a hand mixer on medium-high speed to whip the whipping cream, sugar, and vanilla until stiff peaks form. Serve each cupcake with a generous spoonful of fresh strawberries and a dollop of whipped cream.

Cinnamon Oatmeal Cupcakes with Raisins and Walnuts

Just like any hearty bowl of oatmeal, these cupcakes are packed with plenty of oats, raisins, walnuts, and cinnamon. Instead of frosting, I top them with the same crunchy, sweet oat topping used in the Apple Crisp Caramel Cupcakes (page 44). But if you're a frosting fiend, I surely won't judge you for whipping up a batch of vanilla or cinnamon buttercream to go on top.

MAKES 18 CUPCAKES

OATMEAL TOPPING
3/4 cup rolled oats
1/2 cup walnuts, chopped
1/2 cup (1 stick) unsalted butter, at room
    temperature
2 tablespoons unbleached all-purpose flour
2 tablespoons light brown sugar
2 teaspoons ground cinnamon
Pinch of salt

CUPCAKES
3/4 cup raisins
3/4 cup (1 1/2 sticks) unsalted butter, at room
    temperature
1 1/2 cups granulated sugar
3 large eggs
2 teaspoons vanilla extract
2 teaspoons baking powder
1/2 teaspoon baking soda
1/4 teaspoon salt
2 teaspoons ground cinnamon
1 teaspoon ground cloves

2 1/2 cups unbleached all-purpose flour
1 1/3 cups whole milk
3/4 cup rolled oats

1. To make the oatmeal topping, place all the ingredients in a small bowl and use your hands or a fork to mix the ingredients together until evenly combined and crumbly. Set aside.

2. To make the cupcakes, preheat the oven to 350°F and line 2 standard muffin tins with 18 paper liners. Place the raisins in a small bowl and cover them with hot (not boiling) water. Set aside. Use a stand mixer fitted with the paddle attachment or a hand mixer on medium speed to combine the butter and sugar for 90 seconds, until fluffy. Add the eggs, one at a time, mixing in each egg completely before adding the next. Use a spatula to scrape down the sides of the bowl. Then, with the mixer on medium-low speed, add the vanilla, baking powder, baking soda, and salt. Mix for about 30 seconds, then

add the cinnamon and cloves. Turn the mixer up to medium-high speed and mix for another 30 seconds, until all the ingredients are combined well. Finally, add the flour, ½ cup at a time, alternately with the milk, ⅓ cup at a time, mixing until each addition is fully incorporated before adding the next. Scrape down the sides of the bowl again and continue to mix the batter on medium-high speed for 30 seconds, until smooth and creamy. Drain the raisins really well and, using a spatula or wooden spoon, fold the raisins and oats into the batter until just combined.

3. Pour the batter into the prepared cups so they're two-thirds full. Spoon a heaping teaspoon of the crumbly topping over the batter and bake for about 25 minutes, or until the edges of the cupcakes have started to turn golden brown and the cake around the sides of the crumbly mixture is set (it'll bounce back when you gently press your finger into it). Allow the cupcakes to rest in the tins for 10 minutes before transferring them to a wire rack to cool a little more. Best when served warm.

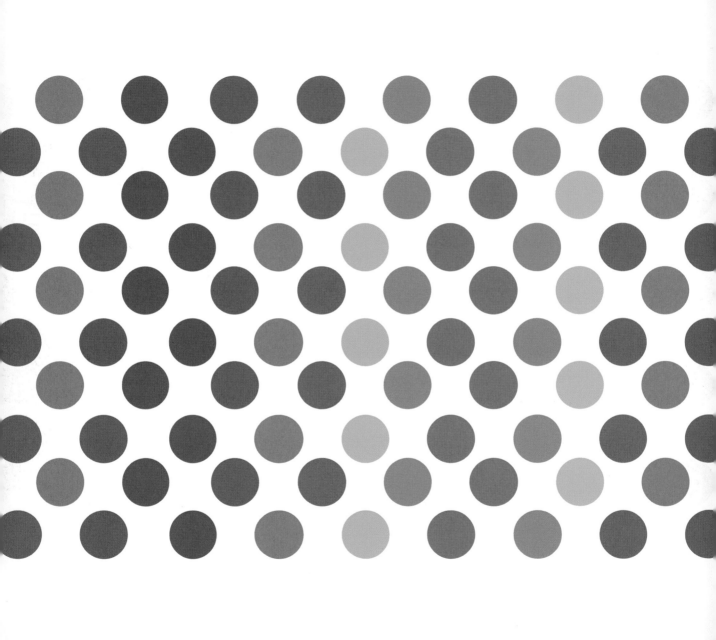

Chapter 4

I WANT CANDY!

Okay, you probably only need to flip through this book for about 2½ seconds to conclude that I have a major—MAJOR—sweet tooth. And if you've made it to Chapter 4, chances are you do, too. As soon as my *Bake It in a Cupcake* adventures began, I started experimenting with some of my favorite candies. Nerds, peanut butter cups, Twix bars—you name it, I've baked it into a cake. As I mentioned in the Introduction, not everything has worked (Starburst candies, for example, have caused me to throw slightly embarrassing hissy fits in the kitchen on a number of occasions), but there are some candies that work so well inside these recipes that I'm not completely convinced this wasn't their purpose all along. This chapter holds some of the best recipes from my hours of candy-filled research; so get ready—your sweet tooth is about to be taken to a new, completely epic level of sweet . . . without the embarrassing hissy fits.

Fruity Rainbow Cupcakes with Toasted Meringue

The delicate fruity flavor in these cupcakes comes from an extra dose of sugar by way of candy-filled straws like Pixy Stix. And that's only half the fun—thanks to a little food coloring, the finished cupcakes look like fluffy pastel rainbows, especially after being topped with a light, sweet cloud of homemade meringue.

MAKES 18 CUPCAKES

CUPCAKES

¾ cup (1½ sticks) unsalted butter, at room
   temperature
1½ cups granulated sugar
3 large eggs
2 teaspoons vanilla extract
2 teaspoons baking powder
½ teaspoon baking soda
¼ teaspoon salt
2½ cups unbleached all-purpose flour
1⅓ cups whole milk
1 (48-stick) bag Pixy Stix or similar candy straws
   in assorted flavors
Food coloring

MERINGUE

4 egg whites
1 cup superfine or castor sugar

1. To make the cupcakes, preheat the oven to 350°F and line 2 standard muffin tins with 18 paper liners. Use a stand mixer fitted with the paddle attachment or a hand mixer on medium speed to combine the butter and sugar for 90 seconds, until fluffy. Add the eggs, one at a time, mixing in each egg completely before adding the next. Use a spatula to scrape down the sides of the bowl. Then, with the mixer on medium-low speed, add the vanilla, baking powder, baking soda, and salt. Turn the mixer up to medium-high speed and mix for an additional 30 seconds, until all the ingredients are well combined. Finally, add the flour, ½ cup at a time, alternately with the milk, ⅓ cup at a time, mixing until each addition is fully incorporated before adding the next. Scrape down the sides of the bowl again and continue to mix the batter on medium-high speed for 30 seconds, until smooth and creamy.

continued on page 79 ⮕

2. Divide the batter evenly among 5 small bowls (or however many different flavors/colors you want in your cupcakes). Empty the contents of 7 sugar-filled sticks of one flavor into each bowl (you'll have sticks left over) and use a spoon to stir the flavored sugar into the batter. Because the sugar itself isn't very colorful, I like to add a few drops of food coloring to each bowl in corresponding colors—purple for grape, red for cherry, etc.

3. Spoon the different-colored batter into the tins, one layer at a time, until the cups are about three-quarters full. Bake for 22 to 24 minutes, or until the edges of the cupcakes have started to turn golden brown and the cake springs back when you gently press your finger into the top of it. (Since there's nothing in the center of these cupcakes, you can also use the toothpick test—just stick a clean toothpick into the center of the cupcake; if it comes out clean, they're done.) Allow the cupcakes to rest in the tins for 10 minutes before transferring them to a wire rack to finish cooling.

4. To make the meringue, begin by putting 2 cups water into a medium saucepan and bring it to a boil over medium-high heat. Pour the egg whites and sugar into a heatproof bowl and place the bowl over the saucepan. The bottom of the bowl should not be touching the water (it's okay if it's close, though). Stir the egg whites until the sugar has dissolved. Once the mixture has reached 140° to 150°F, remove the egg whites from the heat and use a stand mixer with the whisk attachment or a hand mixer to beat the egg whites on high speed until soft peaks begin to form. Pipe or spread a generous helping of the meringue on top of each cooled cupcake (see page 137). If you'd like, toast the meringue under the broiler for a minute or two, until the peaks start to brown (it'll make your kitchen smell like cotton candy!).

The Elvis: Peanut Butter-Banana Cupcakes

I suppose if you really want to call these peanut butter and banana cupcakes the "Elvis," you'd have to throw some bacon on top—which you can do! Just fry up a few slices of thick-cut bacon, allow them to cool, then crumble the bacon bits over the cupcakes after you've frosted them. Salty, chocolate, smoky—delicious. If you don't like the idea of having bacon for dessert, though, you can finish the cupcakes off with a generous pinch of miniature chocolate chips. They're just as good without the pig, I promise. Even Elvis would approve.

MAKES 22 CUPCAKES

CUPCAKES

¾ cup (1½ sticks) unsalted butter, at room temperature
1½ cups granulated sugar
3 large eggs
2 teaspoons vanilla extract
2 teaspoons baking powder
½ teaspoon baking soda
½ teaspoon salt
2 ripe bananas, mashed (about 1 cup)
2½ cups unbleached all-purpose flour
1⅓ cups whole milk
22 regular-size chocolate peanut butter cups

FROSTING

1¼ cups (2½ sticks) unsalted butter, at room temperature
2 cups powdered sugar
3 tablespoons dark chocolate cocoa powder
1 to 3 tablespoons whole milk, as needed
½ cup miniature chocolate chips, for garnish
3 slices thick-cut bacon, cooked, for garnish

1. To make the cupcakes, preheat the oven to 350°F and line 2 standard muffin tins with 22 paper liners. Using a stand mixer fitted with the paddle attachment or a hand mixer on medium speed, blend the butter and sugar together for about 90 seconds, until fluffy. Add the eggs, one at time, mixing in each egg completely before adding the next. With the mixer on medium-low speed, add the vanilla, baking powder, baking soda, and salt. Turn the mixer up to medium-high speed and mix for an additional 30 seconds, until all the ingredients are well combined. Add the mashed bananas and mix for 30 more seconds. Finally, add the flour, ½ cup at a time, alternately with the milk, ⅓ cup at a time, mixing until each addition is fully incorporated before adding the next. Continue to mix the batter on medium-high speed for 30 seconds, until the batter is smooth. It's fine if there are small lumps of banana.

2. Spoon 2 heaping tablespoons of batter into each cup in the prepared tins. Place a peanut butter cup on top of the batter and then cover with another heaping tablespoon of batter so the cups are about three-quarters full. Bake for about 24 minutes, until the cupcakes have started to turn golden brown on the edges and the cake springs back when you gently press your finger into the top of it. Allow them to rest for 10 minutes in the tins and then transfer to a wire rack to cool completely.

3. To make the frosting, whip the butter for about 30 seconds with a stand mixer fitted with the whisk attachment or a hand mixer on medium speed. Add the powdered sugar, ½ cup at a time, and the cocoa powder, whipping on medium-high speed until fluffy. With the mixer on medium speed, drizzle in 1 tablespoon of the milk. If the frosting is still really thick, you can use another tablespoon or two of milk to reach the desired consistency. You should be able to easily spread or pipe the frosting onto the cooled cupcakes, but it should not be runny at all. Give the cupcakes an extra dose of chocolate by sprinkling some miniature chocolate chips on top (or bacon, if you dare).

Cherry Cordial Brownie Cupcakes with White Chocolate Truffle Frosting

As soon as I tasted the white chocolate truffle frosting I made for these brownie cupcakes, I wanted to put it on everything. It was so good that it made me regret every cupcake I'd ever baked and topped with anything other than this frosting. My infatuation has since subsided a little bit, but only because now I know it's a frosting so good that it should be reserved for very special occasions, like the kind of occasion that calls for a cherry cordial–filled brownie.

MAKES 12 BROWNIE CUPCAKES

BROWNIES

4 ounces unsweetened chocolate, broken or
    chopped into small pieces
¾ cup (1½ sticks) unsalted butter
2 cups granulated sugar
3 large eggs
1 teaspoon vanilla extract
½ teaspoon salt
1 cup unbleached all-purpose flour
12 chocolate cherry cordial candies

FROSTING

15 white chocolate truffles, such as Lindor
    truffles
2 tablespoons whole milk
1 cup (2 sticks) unsalted butter, at room
    temperature
2 cups powdered sugar
Chocolate sprinkles or chocolate shavings,
    for garnish (optional)

1. Preheat the oven to 350°F and line a standard muffin tin with 12 paper liners. Place the chocolate and butter in a medium microwave-safe bowl and microwave the ingredients on high for 90 seconds, stopping halfway through to stir the butter and chocolate together. After 90 seconds, continue to stir the butter and chocolate until all the chocolate chunks have completely melted into the butter. (If you microwave any longer, you risk burning the chocolate, so it's best to be patient and let the chocolate melt slowly while you stir.) Using a wooden spoon, stir in the granulated sugar. It will be thick and grainy, and the sugar should be distributed evenly. Next, stir in the eggs one at a time until the mixture is smooth. Add the vanilla and salt and stir for an additional 20 seconds, until they're both incorporated. Finally, mix in the flour until just combined, taking care not to overstir.

2. Put a heaping tablespoon of brownie batter into each cup in the prepared tin. Place an unwrapped chocolate cherry cordial in each tin, pressing it gently into the batter, and then top the cherry cordial with more batter so the top and the sides are completely covered. The cups should be about three-quarters full. Bake the brownies for 23 to 25 minutes, until they have begun to set. Begin checking for doneness at 20 minutes, as ovens vary. You can test by sticking a toothpick into the side of the brownie—if it comes out clean, they're done. Be careful not to overbake, though, or your brownies will be dry. Allow the brownies to cool in the tin for 10 minutes, then transfer them to a wire rack to cool completely.

3. To make the frosting, place the truffles and milk in a small microwave-safe bowl. Microwave on high for 20 seconds, then stir. Microwave on high for another 20 seconds and stir again until the white chocolate and milk have melted together into a smooth mixture. Set aside to cool while you make the rest of the frosting. Whip the butter for about 30 seconds with a stand mixer fitted with the whisk attachment or a hand mixer on medium speed. Add the powdered sugar, ½ cup at a time, whipping on medium-high speed until fluffy. Once the white chocolate mixture is cool (or slightly warm) to the touch, drizzle it into the butter mixture with the mixer on medium-high speed. Continue to whip for 20 seconds or so, until the white chocolate is well combined and the frosting is fluffy. Pipe or spread the frosting on top of the cooled cupcakes (see page 137) and, if you'd like, top with some chocolate sprinkles or chocolate shavings for garnish.

Caramel Cookie Brownie Cupcakes

Twix or any Twix-like candy bar is the star of this show. I prefer caramel, but maybe you like peanut butter. That's okay. And if you're looking to make something not cupcake shaped, you can bake this recipe as a pan of brownies—just make the brownie batter, pour it into a greased 9-inch square pan, and arrange a single layer of 24 miniature Twix candy bars ½ inch or so apart on top. Bake for 24 minutes, until the brownies have set, and allow them to cool completely before cutting (although I'm sure no one will notice if a little tiny piece of the corner is missing . . . hint hint).

MAKES 12 BROWNIE CUPCAKES

BROWNIES
4 ounces unsweetened chocolate, broken or
   chopped into small pieces
¾ cup (1½ sticks) unsalted butter
2 cups granulated sugar
3 large eggs
1 teaspoon vanilla extract
½ teaspoon salt
1 cup unbleached all-purpose flour
24 miniature chocolate-covered caramel cookies,
   such as Twix bars

CARAMEL TOPPING
20 bite-sized caramel candies
2 tablespoons heavy cream

1. To make the brownies, preheat the oven to 350°F and line 2 standard muffin tins with 12 paper liners. Place the chocolate and butter in a medium microwave-safe bowl and microwave on high for 90 seconds, stopping halfway through to stir the butter and chocolate together. After 90 seconds, continue to stir the butter and chocolate until all the chocolate chunks have completely melted into the butter. (If you microwave any longer, you risk burning the chocolate, so it's best to be patient and let the chocolate melt slowly while you stir.) Using a wooden spoon, stir in the granulated sugar. It will be thick and grainy, and the sugar should be distributed evenly. Next, stir in the eggs one at a time until the mixture is smooth. Add the vanilla and salt and stir for an additional 20 seconds, until they're both incorporated. Finally, mix in the flour until just combined, taking care not to overstir.

2. Put a heaping tablespoon of brownie batter into each cup in the prepared tins. Place 2 caramel cookie bars side by side in each cup, pressing them gently into the batter, and then top them with more batter so the top and the sides of the cookies are completely covered. The cups should be about three-quarters full. Bake the brownies for 23 to 25 minutes, until they have begun to set. Begin checking for doneness at 20 minutes, as ovens vary. Be careful not to overbake, though, or your brownies will be dry. Allow the brownies to cool in the tins for 10 minutes, then transfer them to a wire rack to cool completely.

3. To make the caramel topping, place the unwrapped caramel candies in a small microwave-safe bowl. Pour the cream over the caramels and microwave on high for 20 seconds. Stir the mixture (it will be thick) and continue to microwave on high for 20-second increments until the caramel is smooth and the cream is well incorporated. It will take about 60 seconds total. Allow the mixture to cool for 5 to 10 minutes so it thickens slightly. Dip the tops of the cooled brownies into the caramel, allow some excess to drip away, and then place the brownies right side up back on a wire rack to allow the caramel to set. It will probably drip down the sides a bit—that's okay! It's a small price to pay for ooey gooey goodness.

Chocolate-Covered Pretzel Brownie Bites with Salted Caramel Frosting

Sometimes it's nearly impossible to choose between a salty and a sweet snack, and with these brownie bites you don't have to! I like to use candy-coated chocolate-covered pretzel pieces, like Pretzel M&M's, but you could use your favorite chocolate-covered pretzels, too. Just be sure to break them into bite-sized pieces.

MAKES 36 MINIATURE BROWNIE CUPCAKES

BROWNIES

4 ounces unsweetened chocolate, broken or
  chopped into small pieces
¾ cup (1½ sticks) unsalted butter
2 cups granulated sugar
3 large eggs
1 teaspoon vanilla extract
½ teaspoon salt
1 cup unbleached all-purpose flour
1 (9.9-ounce) bag pretzel M&M's or similar
  chocolate-covered pretzel pieces, plus more
  for garnish

FROSTING

15 to 20 bite-sized caramel candies
2 tablespoons heavy cream
2 sticks (1 cup) unsalted butter, at room
  temperature
2 cups powdered sugar
1 tablespoon kosher salt

1. To make the brownies, preheat the oven to 350°F and line 2 miniature muffin tins with 36 paper liners. Place the chocolate and butter in a medium microwave-safe bowl and microwave the ingredients on high for 90 seconds, stopping halfway through to stir the butter and chocolate together. After 90 seconds, continue to stir the butter and chocolate until all the chocolate chunks have completely melted into the butter. (If you microwave any longer, you risk burning the chocolate, so it's best to be patient and let the chocolate melt slowly while you stir.) Using a wooden spoon, stir in the granulated sugar. It will be thick and grainy, and the sugar should be distributed evenly. Next, stir in the eggs one at a time until the mixture is smooth. Add the vanilla and salt and stir for an additional 20 seconds, until they're both incorporated. Finally, mix in the flour until just combined, taking care not to overstir.

continued on page 88 ➡

2. Using a 1-inch cookie scoop, spoon the brownie batter into each cup in the prepared tins, so they're about three-quarters full. Press a few chocolate-covered pretzel pieces into the top of each brownie, nestling them into the batter but not covering them. Bake for about 20 minutes, or until the brownies have set and a toothpick inserted into the center of a brownie comes out clean. (Take care not to overbake or your brownies could be quite dry.) Allow the brownies to cool in the tins for 10 minutes before transferring them to a wire rack to finish cooling.

3. To make the frosting, place all the unwrapped caramel candies in a small microwave-safe bowl. Pour the cream over the caramels and microwave on high for 20 seconds. Stir the mixture (it will be thick) and continue to microwave on high for 20-second increments until the caramel is smooth and the cream is well incorporated. It will take about 60 seconds total. Place the mixture in the refrigerator to cool. Using a stand mixer fitted with the whisk attachment or a hand mixer on medium speed, whip the butter for 30 seconds, until creamy. Add the powdered sugar, ½ cup at a time, whipping at medium speed until fluffy. After the caramel has cooled in the refrigerator for 10 minutes—it's okay if it's still a little warm to the touch—set aside a few teaspoons to use as a garnish later. Then give the remaining caramel mixture a stir and, with the mixer on medium speed, slowly drizzle it into the frosting. If the caramel is too hot, it will begin to melt the frosting. If this happens, let the caramel cool for a bit longer before continuing. Finally, add the salt a teaspoon at a time, tasting after each addition to ensure you don't add too much. I usually add about a tablespoon (3 teaspoons), but you may like more or less salt. Top each cooled brownie bite with a generous dollop of frosting, an extra pretzel piece, and a drizzle of some of the reserved caramel sauce.

Malted Milk Ball Cupcakes with Malted Chocolate Frosting

There was a week or so when I was adding malted milk powder to everything I baked. Malted cookies, malted chocolate cupcakes, malted vanilla buttercream . . . I was one nervous breakdown away from sprinkling malted milk powder on my toothbrush in the morning. If you have had a similar relationship with malt powder, then meet your new best friend, Malted Milk Ball Cupcakes with Malted Chocolate Frosting.

MAKES 18 CUPCAKES

CUPCAKES

1 (12-ounce) bag malted milk balls, such as
   Whoppers
¾ cup (1½ sticks) unsalted butter, at room
   temperature
1½ cups granulated sugar
3 large eggs
2 teaspoons vanilla extract
2 teaspoons baking powder
½ teaspoon baking soda
¼ teaspoon salt
3 tablespoons malted milk powder
2½ cups unbleached all-purpose flour
1⅓ cups whole milk

FROSTING

4 ounces unsweetened chocolate, broken or
   chopped into small pieces
2 to 4 tablespoons whole milk, as needed
1 cup (2 sticks) unsalted butter, at room
   temperature
2 cups powdered sugar
2 tablespoons malted milk powder

1. To make the cupcakes, preheat the oven to 350°F and line 2 standard muffin tins with 18 paper liners. Pour half of the malted milk balls into a plastic bag and use a rolling pin or meat tenderizer to crush the candies into large chunks. Set them aside. Use a stand mixer fitted with the paddle attachment or a hand mixer on medium speed to combine the butter and sugar for 90 seconds, until fluffy. Add the eggs, one at a time, mixing in each egg completely before adding the next. Use a spatula to scrape down the side of the bowl.

continued on page 91

With the mixer on medium-low speed, add the vanilla, baking powder, baking soda, and salt. Turn the mixer up to medium-high speed and mix for an additional 30 seconds, until all the ingredients are well combined. Add the malted milk powder and mix for an additional 15 or 20 seconds. Finally, add the flour, ½ cup at a time, alternating with the milk, ⅓ cup at a time, mixing until each addition is fully incorporated before adding the next. Scrape down the sides of the bowl again and then continue to mix the batter on medium-high speed for 30 seconds, until smooth and creamy. Pour the crushed malted milk balls into the batter and stir with a wooden spoon until just combined.

2. Pour the batter into the prepared tins so the cups are about three-quarters full. Bake for about 25 minutes, until the edges and tops of the cupcakes have turned golden brown and the cake springs back when you gently press your finger into the top of it. Allow the cupcakes to cool in the tins for at least 10 minutes before moving them to a wire rack to finish cooling.

3. To make the frosting, place the chocolate and 2 tablespoons of the milk in a small microwave-safe bowl and microwave on high for 20 seconds. Stir and microwave for another 20 seconds. Continue to stir the mixture until the chocolate has completely melted and the milk is fully incorporated. Place the bowl in the refrigerator so it can cool while you prepare the rest of the frosting. Whip the butter for about 30 seconds with a stand mixer fitted with the whisk attachment or a hand mixer on medium speed. Add the powdered sugar, ½ cup at a time, whipping on medium-high speed until fluffy. Add the malted milk powder and whip for another 20 seconds or so, until combined. Once the chocolate mixture is cool to the touch (slightly warm is okay), give it another stir and drizzle it into the frosting while whipping on medium-high speed. Continue to mix until combined. If the frosting is too thick, add the remaining 2 tablespoons milk and whip until fluffy. Pipe or spread the frosting on top of the cooled cupcakes (see page 137) and top with the remaining malted milk balls.

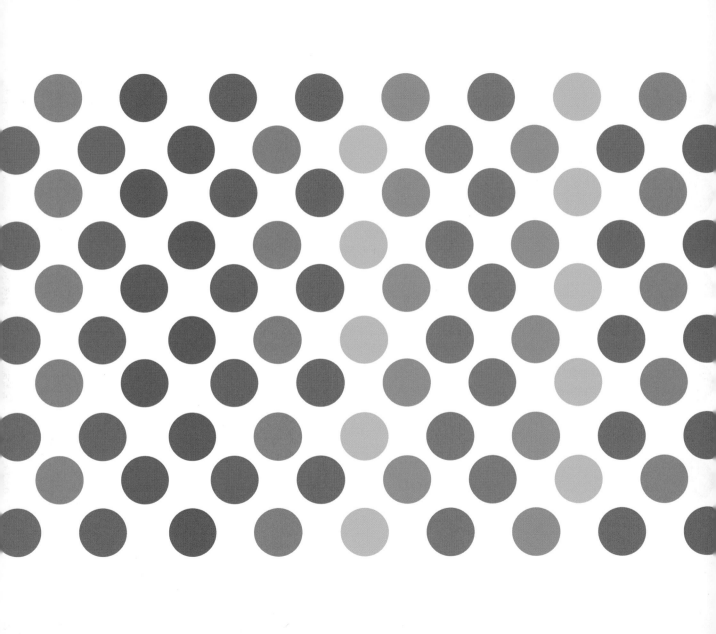

Chapter 5

SAVORY TREATS

Even the most ravenous sugar addict needs to take a break from sweets now and then, which is why I am so excited about all these savory recipes. Also, I LOVE cheese, so I just had to include some savory snacks to accommodate some of my favorite cheeses—Gorgonzola, Swiss, Brie . . . insert drooling noises here. Just like every cupcake recipe in this book, these savory recipes lend themselves to your personalization. For example, don't like Brie cheese? Try the Brie-Stuffed Apricot Cornmeal Muffins (opposite,) with Stilton instead. Or if you're a bacon fanatic, throw some bacon bits into the Egg-Filled Croissant Cups (page 99). Don't be afraid to take a chance and try something a little different. That is, after all, how *Bake It in a Cupcake* was born.

Brie-Stuffed Apricot Cornmeal Muffins

With the buttery, mild Brie cheese and not-too-sweet dried apricots, these cornmeal muffins benefit from a generous sprinkle of freshly cracked black pepper. It will really help bring out the flavors of the apricots and cheese. And if you're feeling experimental, you can try this recipe with various herbs. They're great with rosemary, for example, and they'd also taste delicious with a few teaspoons of fresh thyme or maybe even sage. Fresh herbs and fancy cheese—I like to think of this as the sophisticated side of *Bake It in a Cupcake*.

MAKES 12 MUFFINS

12 to 24 dried apricots (depending on size)

1 small wheel Brie cheese (1½ to 2 pounds)

1½ cups unbleached all-purpose flour

⅔ cup granulated sugar

⅔ cup cornmeal

1 tablespoon baking powder

½ teaspoon salt, plus more for garnish

½ teaspoon freshly cracked black pepper, plus
  more for garnish

1 cup whole milk

3 large eggs

⅓ cup vegetable oil

3 tablespoons unsalted butter, melted

1. First, stuff the apricots with the Brie. Open a dried apricot at the seam (where it was cut open to remove the pit) and place a small hunk of cheese (about 1 teaspoon) in the center of the fruit. Fold the apricot back over the cheese and repeat until all the apricots have been stuffed. If your apricots are smaller, you can use 2 of them for each chunk of cheese—you don't need to completely seal the fruit closed, but you don't want to leave too much room for the cheese to escape, either. Set the stuffed apricots aside.

continued on page 97 ➡

2. To make the muffins, preheat the oven to 350°F and butter or spray nonstick baking spray into one standard muffin tin. Combine the flour, sugar, cornmeal, baking powder, salt, and pepper in a medium bowl and whisk until well combined. In another medium bowl, combine the milk, eggs, oil, and melted butter and whisk until well combined. Slowly pour the wet ingredients into the dry ingredients, while slowly whisking at the same time. Continue to stir until just combined.

3. Spoon the batter into the prepared muffin tin so the cups are about two-thirds full. Place a piece of stuffed fruit in the center of each muffin cup and gently press it into the batter. Use a spoon or your finger to spread the batter over the fruit. Sprinkle the top of each muffin with a small pinch of salt and pepper, to taste. Bake for 20 to 25 minutes, until the edges of the muffins have started to brown and the muffins spring back when you gently press your finger into the tops of them. Allow them to cool in the tin for at least 5 minutes before removing. Serve warm, while the cheese is still a bit gooey.

Pear and Gorgonzola Muffins

Okay, you caught me. Technically, this is the same vanilla cupcake batter recipe seen throughout this book. But since we're excluding the vanilla extract and the frosting, and adding a generous and surprising dose of sharp Gorgonzola cheese, I count these muffins as a savory snack. Which means you can have one for breakfast, or have one with dinner, and *still* have a cupcake for dessert. Smart, right?

MAKES 18 MUFFINS

¾ cup (1½ sticks) unsalted butter, at room temperature

1½ cups granulated sugar

3 large eggs

2 teaspoons baking powder

½ teaspoon baking soda

¼ teaspoon salt

2½ cups unbleached all-purpose flour

1⅓ cups whole milk

2 medium pears, peeled, cored, and cut into 1-inch cubes

½ cup crumbled Gorgonzola cheese, plus more for garnish

Salt and freshly ground black pepper, to taste

1. To make the muffins, preheat the oven to 350°F and line a standard muffin tin with 18 paper liners. Use a stand mixer fitted with the paddle attachment or a hand mixer on medium speed to combine the butter and sugar for 90 seconds, until fluffy. Add the eggs, one at a time, mixing in each egg completely before adding the next. Use a spatula to scrape down the side of the bowl. With the mixer on medium-low speed, add the baking powder, baking soda, and salt. Turn the mixer up to medium-high speed and mix for an additional 30 seconds, so all the ingredients are well combined. Finally, add the flour, ½ cup at a time, alternately with the milk, ⅓ cup at a time, mixing until each addition is fully incorporated before adding the next. Scrape down the sides of the bowl again and then continue to mix the batter on medium-high speed for 30 seconds, until smooth and creamy. Use a wooden spoon to stir in the pears and Gorgonzola cheese crumbles.

2. Fill each cup in the prepared muffin tin so they are about three-quarters full. Sprinkle a pinch of extra Gorgonzola on top of the muffins and bake for about 25 minutes, until the edges and tops of the muffins have turned golden brown and the cake springs back when you gently press your finger into the top of it. Allow the muffins to cool in the tin for at least 10 minutes before moving to a wire rack. Sprinkle with salt and pepper to taste, and serve warm or at room temperature.

Egg-Filled Croissant Cups with Swiss Cheese and Chives

Don't panic! I am not about to ask you to make your own croissant dough from scratch to enjoy these buttery, cheesy, egg-filled croissant pockets. That's a whole different book. This specific recipe can be made easily with some of your favorite store-bought croissant dough found in your local grocer's refrigerated section (next to the pie crust you use to "cheat with" when making the Pumpkin Pie Cupcakes on page 130). Pair these right out of the oven with some fruit and a green salad for an easy brunch, then store the extras in the refrigerator for lunch the next day.

MAKES 6 CROISSANT CUPS

1 (8-ounce) tube premade croissant dough

6 slices Swiss cheese (3- or 4-inch squares work fine, but you can use more if you like a lot of cheese)

Salt and freshly ground black pepper

6 eggs

¼ cup chopped fresh chives

1. Preheat the oven to 375°F and spray 6 muffin cups with nonstick baking spray. Open the tube of croissant dough and roll it out onto a lightly floured surface. It will be perforated for croissants, and we want to eliminate holes while working with the dough as little as possible (overworking the dough will make it tough). Dust your hands with a little bit of flour so they don't stick to the dough and lightly pat the perforations out of the dough. Use a sharp knife to cut the dough into 6 equal squares. Place one square of dough into each muffin cup and press it into the cup to completely cover the bottom and sides of the cup. Press the dough so a little bit sticks up over the edges of the cup—that edge will help hold the egg in.

continued on page 101 ➡

2. Put a slice of Swiss cheese in the bottom of each dough cup and sprinkle with just a bit of salt and black pepper. Crack one egg into each muffin cup. I prefer to use a fork or a chopstick to break the yolk and *lightly* beat the egg, but you can skip this step if you'd like your yolks to remain intact. Sprinkle the eggs with some of the chives, salt, and pepper and place the pan in the oven. Bake for 20 to 24 minutes, until the edges of the pastry have turned a deep golden brown and the egg has completely set. I prefer a medium-hard yolk, so I bake the croissant cups until they no longer jiggle but the yolk is still soft to the touch—remember, the egg will continue to cook a little bit longer when out of the oven but still in the tin. Allow the cups to rest in the tin for about 5 minutes before serving.

Chili- and Cheddar-Filled Biscuits

Not everything in this book requires double the work. In fact, these chili biscuit cups are super easy since they use just a few premade ingredients. Literally three ingredients. Of course, if you have a trusty biscuit recipe or a tried-and-true chili recipe, I'm sure your personal touch would make these savory cups even more delicious; but these shortcuts will do just fine when you need a quick dinner for someone like me, who believes food is most fun to eat when it's cup shaped.

MAKES 16 BISCUITS

1 (16-ounce) tube large biscuits, such as Pillsbury Grands
½ cup shredded sharp cheddar cheese
1 (15-ounce) can chili

1. Preheat the oven to 350°F. Butter or spray with nonstick baking spray 16 cups in 2 standard muffin tins. Open the tube of biscuit dough and separate each biscuit onto a cutting board. Using a sharp knife, carefully slice the biscuits in half, lengthwise, so you have 16 disks of dough. Press one disk of dough into each prepared muffin cup, covering the bottom and the sides of the cup without stretching the biscuit too thin.

2. Sprinkle a teaspoon of shredded cheddar cheese into the bottom of each biscuit cup. Spoon the chili on top of the cheese so the cups are three-quarters full and bake for 12 minutes, until the biscuits have risen and the edges have started to turn golden brown. Remove them from the oven and sprinkle another teaspoon of cheese over the chili. Place them back in the oven for a minute or two, until the cheese has melted. Allow the cups to rest in the tin for about 5 minutes before serving.

Jalapeño Popper–Filled Corn Muffins

Jalapeño poppers, small jalapeño chiles stuffed with cream cheese and then fried to golden perfection, are one of my very favorite bar food snacks, second only to mozzarella sticks. And now that I think about it, this recipe would be great with those, too. I use premade poppers, which you can find in the frozen section of most supermarkets. (Whenever I fry things at home my house smells like old oil for two weeks and, well, gross.) One tip: When preparing the poppers for this recipe, bake them instead of fry so they aren't too greasy. And if I were you, I would make some extras, because chances are you'll need a snack while you prepare the batter.

MAKES 12 MUFFINS

1½ cups unbleached all-purpose flour

⅔ cup granulated sugar

⅔ cup cornmeal

1 tablespoon baking powder

½ teaspoon salt

½ teaspoon freshly ground black pepper

1 cup whole milk

3 large eggs

⅓ cup vegetable oil

3 tablespoons unsalted butter, melted

6 frozen jalapeño poppers, made as directed on the box and cut in half widthwise

1. Preheat the oven to 350°F and butter or spray with nonstick baking spray into 12 cups in a standard muffin tin. Combine the flour, sugar, cornmeal, baking powder, salt, and black pepper) in a medium bowl and whisk until well combined. In another medium bowl, combine the milk, eggs, oil, and melted butter and whisk until combined. Slowly pour the wet ingredients into the dry ingredients while slowly whisking. Continue to stir until just combined.

2. Spoon the batter into the prepared muffin cups so the cups are about two-thirds full. Place one jalapeño popper in the center of each muffin cup and gently press it into the batter. Use a spoon or your finger to spread the batter over the popper so it is completely covered. Bake for 20 to 25 minutes, until the edges of the muffins have started to brown and the muffins spring back when you gently press your finger into the tops of them. Allow them to cool in the tin for at least 5 minutes before removing. Serve warm.

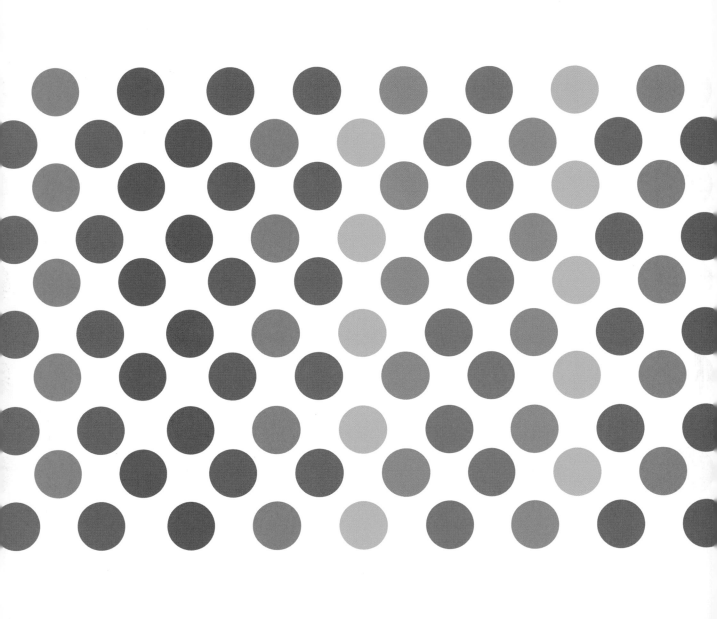

Chapter 6

SEASONAL AND HOLIDAY FAVORITES

I am a holiday fanatic. There's something about holidays—*all* holidays—that turns me into a giddy child. The lights at Christmastime, all the food and family at Thanksgiving, scary movies at Halloween—I even love the goofiest and perhaps most pointless holiday of all, Valentine's Day. Perhaps it's all the candy, now that I think about it . . . Anyway, this chapter holds all the *Bake It in a Cupcake* holiday recipes, including the two most requested recipes, the pumpkin pie–filled cupcakes (page 130) and the heart-filled cupcakes (opposite). I'm also finally sharing with you some holiday recipes that have never been seen before, like the All-American Apple Pie for the Fourth of July Cupcakes (page 121) and the Girl Scout Cookie Cupcakes (page 111).

Don't feel like you can only enjoy these treats once a year. So long as you can get your hands on some of the seasonal ingredients, you should feel free to make any of these cupcakes whenever you want. Rules are for fools. (But good luck finding eggnog in July.)

Pink Heart-Filled Cupcakes with Strawberry Taffy Frosting

These vanilla bean cupcakes really have heart. Cut or bite into one to see how much love went into them. The best part: They're surprisingly simple. And if your sweetheart happens to be a chocolate fan, you could just as easily bake your heart into some chocolate cake batter (see page 16). If you go that route, I recommend finishing them off with a generous spoonful of decadent ganache (see page 29) for a true death-by-chocolate experience.

MAKES 12 CUPCAKES

CUPCAKES

¾ cup (1½ sticks) unsalted butter, at room
    temperature
1½ cups granulated sugar
3 large eggs
Seeds from 1 vanilla bean (see page 63)
2 teaspoons baking powder
½ teaspoon baking soda
¼ teaspoon salt
2½ cups unbleached all-purpose flour
1⅓ cups whole milk
Red food coloring

FROSTING

10 bite-sized pieces strawberry taffy
2 tablespoons heavy cream
1 cup (2 sticks) unsalted butter, at room
    temperature
2 cups powdered sugar
12 pieces conversation heart candy

1. To make the cupcakes, preheat the oven to 350°F, use a nontoxic marker to make a small dot on the edge of 12 paper liners, and place them in one standard muffin tin, with all the dots facing the same direction. Use a stand mixer fitted with the paddle attachment or a hand mixer on medium speed to combine the butter and sugar for 90 seconds, until fluffy. Add the eggs, one at a time, mixing in each egg completely before adding the next. With the mixer on medium-low speed, add the vanilla seeds, baking powder, baking soda, and salt. Use a spatula to scrape down the sides of the bowl, then turn the mixer up to medium-high speed and mix for an additional 30 seconds, until all the ingredients are well combined. Finally, add the flour, ½ cup at a time, alternately with the milk, ⅓ cup at a time, mixing until each addition is fully incorporated before adding the next. Scrape down the sides of the bowl one more time and continue to mix

continued on page 109 ➡

the batter on medium-high speed another 30 seconds. It should be smooth and creamy.

2. Pour approximately 1½ cups of the batter into a smaller bowl. This will be for the hearts. Use a spoon to stir in red food coloring, 2 or 3 drops at a time, until you get your desired shade of red or pink. Keep in mind the color will lighten a little while baking. Pour the pink batter into a nonstick or lightly greased 8-inch square baking pan and bake for about 20 minutes, until a toothpick inserted into the center of the cake comes out clean. Allow the cake to cool completely. (It's okay to stick it in the fridge to speed it up—I'm impatient, too.)

3. Once the sheet cake is cool, loosen the cake from the pan by running a knife around the edges of the cake. Carefully invert the pan onto a cutting board. Use a 2-inch heart-shaped cookie cutter to cut out 12 hearts. If you can't find a small heart-shaped cookie cutter, draw a heart on some clean cardboard and use that as a stencil to cut the hearts out with a small knife.

4. Spoon 2 heaping tablespoons of the remaining plain batter into each cup in the prepared tins. Place a heart in each cup, with the bottom of the heart pointing down and the front of the heart facing the dot on the cupcake paper. Press the heart gently into the batter. Cover the top of the heart with a teaspoon of batter. Bake for 24 minutes, or until the edges of the cupcakes have started to turn golden brown and the cake springs back when you gently press your finger into the top of it. Allow the cupcakes to rest in the tins for 10 minutes before transferring them to a wire rack to cool while you make the frosting.

5. To make the frosting, melt the taffy and cream together in a microwave in a small, microwave-safe bowl for 20 seconds on high. Stir and microwave for another 20 seconds, repeating until the mixture has melted. When the taffy mixture is smooth, put the bowl in the fridge so it cools a bit before being added to the frosting (the cream will keep the taffy from hardening).

6. Meanwhile, using a stand mixer with the whisk attachment or a hand mixer, whip the butter for 30 seconds at medium speed until creamy. Add the powdered sugar ½ cup at a time, whipping at medium speed until fluffy. With the mixer on medium-low, drizzle in the cooled taffy cream. Finally, turn the mixer to high and whip the frosting for 30 seconds, until it is pale pink and fluffy. If you'd like the frosting to be a darker shade of pink, add a couple drops of red food coloring. Pipe or spread the frosting on top of the cupcakes (see page 137). Place a candy heart on top of each cupcake, point down, facing in the same direction as the dot on the cupcake wrapper so people will know which way to bite into the cupcake to see the heart. Love!

Conversation Heart Brownie Bites

It takes just one bowl and less than an hour to whip up a batch of these rich, bite-sized brownies. They don't require frosting (you don't want to cover up the sweet messages, after all), but if you want to put a dollop of vanilla frosting on top (see page 116), I certainly won't stop you.

MAKES 36 MINI BROWNIE CUPCAKES

BROWNIES

4 ounces unsweetened chocolate, broken or
   chopped into small pieces
¾ cup (1½ sticks) unsalted butter
2 cups granulated sugar
3 large eggs
½ teaspoon salt
1 teaspoon vanilla extract
1 cup unbleached all-purpose flour
1 cup conversation heart candies, plus more
   for garnish

1. Preheat the oven to 350°F. Line 2 miniature muffin tins with 36 paper liners. Place the chocolate and butter in a medium microwave-safe bowl and microwave on high for 90 seconds, stopping halfway through to stir the butter and chocolate together. After 90 seconds, continue to stir the butter and chocolate until all the chocolate chunks have completely melted into the butter. (If you microwave any longer, you risk burning the chocolate, so it's best to be patient and let the chocolate melt slowly while you stir.) Using a wooden spoon, stir in the granulated sugar. It will be thick and grainy, and the sugar should be distributed evenly. Next, stir in the eggs one at a time until the mixture is smooth. Add the salt and vanilla and stir for an additional 20 seconds, until they're both incorporated. Finally, mix in the flour until just combined, taking care not to overstir.

2. Using a 1-inch cookie scoop, spoon the brownie batter into the prepared cups so they're about three-quarters full. Press a few pieces of heart candy into the top of each brownie (with the words facing up, of course), nestling them into the batter but not covering them. Bake for about 20 minutes, or until the brownies have set and a toothpick inserted into the center of the brownie comes out clean. (Take care not to overbake or your brownies could be quite dry.) Allow the brownies to cool in the tins for 10 minutes before transferring to a wire rack to finish cooling.

Girl Scout Cookie Cupcakes

My favorite season is Girl Scout cookie season. And my favorite Girl Scout cookie is, without a doubt, the Samoa—disks of shortbread covered in caramel, toasted coconut, and chocolate . . . Mmmm. They certainly don't *need* to be improved upon, but baking them into a chocolate cupcake couldn't hurt, right? I top them with chocolate frosting and a sprinkle of toasted coconut. Try not to get any drool on the book.

MAKES 20 CUPCAKES

CUPCAKES

4 ounces unsweetened chocolate, broken or chopped into small pieces

1⅓ cups plus 2 tablespoons whole milk

¾ cup (1½ sticks) unsalted butter, at room temperature

1½ cups granulated sugar

3 large eggs

2 teaspoons vanilla extract

2 teaspoons baking powder

½ teaspoon baking soda

¼ teaspoon salt

½ cup unsweetened cocoa powder

2½ cups unbleached all-purpose flour

20 Samoa Girl Scout cookies

1 cup finely shredded unsweetened coconut, for garnish

FROSTING

2 tablespoons whole milk

4 ounces unsweetened chocolate, broken or chopped into small pieces

1 cup (2 sticks) unsalted butter, at room temperature

2 cups powdered sugar

1. To make the cupcakes, preheat the oven to 350°F and line 2 standard muffin tins with 20 paper liners. Place the chocolate and 2 tablespoons of the milk in a small microwave-safe bowl and microwave for 20 seconds on high. Stir and microwave for another 20 seconds. Stir the mixture until the chocolate has completely melted and the milk is fully incorporated. Place the bowl in the refrigerator to cool while you prepare the rest of the cupcake batter.

continued on page 112 ➡

2. Use a stand mixer fitted with the paddle attachment or a hand mixer on medium speed to combine the butter and sugar for 90 seconds, until fluffy. Add the eggs, one at a time, mixing in each egg completely before adding the next. Use a spatula to scrape down the sides of the bowl. Then, with the mixer on medium-low speed, add the vanilla, baking powder, baking soda, and salt. Add the cocoa powder. Turn the mixer up to medium-high speed and mix for an additional 30 seconds, until all the ingredients are well combined. Scrape down the sides of the bowl. Add the flour, ½ cup at a time, alternately with the remaining 1⅓ cups milk, ⅓ cup at a time, mixing until each addition is fully incorporated before adding the next. Finally, with the mixer on medium-high, drizzle in the cooled chocolate mixture. Continue to mix the batter on medium-high speed for 30 seconds, until smooth and creamy.

3. Spoon 2 heaping tablespoons of batter into each cup in the prepared tins. Place a cookie in each cup and cover with another heaping tablespoon of batter so the top and sides of the cookie are completely covered and the cup is about three-quarters full. Bake for about 25 minutes, until the edges and tops of the cupcakes have set and the cake springs back when you gently press your finger into the top of it. Allow the cupcakes to cool in the tins for at least 10 minutes before moving to a wire rack to cool completely.

4. If you are using toasted coconut as a garnish, leave the oven on and spread the coconut out in a thin layer on a cookie sheet that has been lined with parchment paper. Place in the oven for about 10 minutes, until the coconut has started to turn golden brown.

5. To make the frosting, place 2 tablespoons milk and the chocolate in a small microwave-safe bowl and microwave on high for 20 seconds. Stir and microwave for another 20 seconds. Continue to stir the mixture until the chocolate has completely melted and the milk is fully incorporated. Place the bowl in the refrigerator to cool while you prepare the rest of the frosting.

6. Whip the butter for about 30 seconds with a stand mixer fitted with the whisk attachment or a hand mixer on medium speed. Add the powdered sugar, ½ cup at a time, whipping on medium-high speed until fluffy. Once the chocolate mixture is cool to the touch, give it another stir and drizzle it into the frosting while whipping on medium-high speed. Continue to mix until combined. Pipe or spread the frosting on top of the cooled cupcakes (see page 137) and finish them off with a generous sprinkling of toasted coconut.

 ## VARIATIONS

You can make these cupcakes using any of your favorite Girl Scout Cookies. And you don't have to stick with plain chocolate frosting, either! Here are some frosting alternatives, should you want to experiment. You can even mix and match, you little daredevil.

THIN MINT COOKIES WITH MINT CHOCOLATE FROSTING: Whip a few drops of peppermint extract into the frosting after adding the melted chocolate. And because Thin Mints are so, well, thin, I recommend using 2 cookies in each cupcake instead of one.

TAGALONG COOKIES WITH PEANUT BUTTER CHOCOLATE FROSTING: Whip ½ cup of smooth peanut butter into the butter before you begin to add the powdered sugar.

DULCE DE LECHE COOKIES WITH CHOCOLATE CARAMEL FROSTING: Melt together a handful of caramel candies with a tablespoon of heavy cream. Allow it to cool a bit, then, when it's not too hot to melt the butter, drizzle it into the frosting before adding the chocolate and while mixing at medium-high speed.

The Ultimate Birthday Cake Cupcakes

My friend Jessie Oleson, aka CakeSpy, was the first person to begin championing the Bake It in a Cake blog when it started back in 2010; so when she wrote and released her cookbook, *CakeSpy: Sweet Treats for a Sugar-Filled Life*, she included an ode to Bake It in a Cake by way of cupcake-stuffed cupcakes. Genius, of course! My version has a funfetti-inspired center in a chocolate cupcake and, because there was some vanilla batter left over, I baked off the rest of the cake batter, crumbled it up, and used it as a topping. Cake on a cake filled with cake is the best way to celebrate a birthday.

MAKES 24 CUPCAKES

INNER CUPCAKES
¾ cup (1½ sticks) unsalted butter, at room temperature
1½ cups granulated sugar
3 large eggs
2 teaspoons vanilla extract
2 teaspoons baking powder
½ teaspoon baking soda
¼ teaspoon salt
2½ cups unbleached all-purpose flour
1⅓ cups whole milk
¼ cup rainbow sprinkles

OUTER CUPCAKES
4 ounces unsweetened chocolate, broken or chopped into small pieces
1⅓ cups plus 2 tablespoons whole milk
¾ cup (1½ sticks) unsalted butter, at room temperature
1½ cups granulated sugar
3 large eggs
2 teaspoons vanilla extract
2 teaspoons baking powder
½ teaspoon baking soda
¼ teaspoon salt
½ cup unsweetened cocoa powder
2½ cups unbleached all-purpose flour

FROSTING
1 cup (2 sticks) unsalted butter, at room temperature
2 cups powdered sugar
2 teaspoons vanilla extract
2 tablespoons whole milk, if needed
2 to 3 tablespoons rainbow sprinkles

1. To make the inner cupcakes, preheat the oven to 350°F and spray both a 24-cup miniature muffin tin and a 9-inch square cake pan with nonstick baking spray. Use a stand mixer fitted with the paddle attachment or a hand mixer on medium speed to combine the butter and sugar for 90 seconds, until fluffy. Add the eggs, one at a time, mixing in each egg

continued on page 116 ⇒

completely before adding the next. With the mixer on medium-low speed, add the vanilla, baking powder, baking soda, and salt. Turn the mixer up to medium-high speed and mix for an additional 30 seconds, until all the ingredients are well combined. Finally, add the flour, ½ cup at a time, alternately with the milk, ⅓ cup at a time, mixing until each addition is fully incorporated before adding the next. Continue to mix the batter on medium-high speed for 30 seconds, until smooth and creamy. Use a spatula to fold in the sprinkles until just combined.

2. Spoon the batter into each cup of the prepared miniature cupcake tins so they're about three-quarters full. Pour the remaining batter into the prepared cake pan. Bake for about 25 minutes, until the edges and tops of the cupcakes and the cake have turned golden brown and the cake springs back when you gently press your finger into the top of it. (The cupcakes may bake slightly faster than the cake in the square pan, so keep an eye on the oven.) Allow the cake and the cupcakes to cool in the pans while you prepare the outer cupcakes.

3. To make the outer cupcakes, line 2 standard muffin tins with 24 paper liners. Place the chocolate and 2 tablespoons of the milk in a

small microwave-safe bowl and microwave for 20 seconds on high. Stir and microwave for another 20 seconds. Stir the mixture until the chocolate has completely melted and the milk is fully incorporated. Place the bowl in the refrigerator to cool while you prepare the rest of the cupcake batter.

4. Use a stand mixer fitted with the paddle attachment or a hand mixer on medium speed to combine the butter and sugar for 90 seconds, until fluffy. Add the eggs, one at a time, mixing in each egg completely before adding the next. Use a spatula to scrape down the sides of the bowl. Then, with the mixer on medium-low speed, add the vanilla, baking powder, baking soda, and salt. Add the cocoa powder. Turn the mixer up to medium-high speed and mix for an additional 30 seconds, until all the ingredients are well combined. Scrape down the sides of the bowl and then add the flour, ½ cup at a time, alternately with the remaining 1⅓ cups milk, ⅓ cup at a time, until each addition is fully incorporated before adding the next. Finally, with the mixer on medium-high, drizzle in the cooled chocolate mixture. Continue to mix the batter on medium-high speed for 30 seconds, until smooth and creamy.

5. Spoon a heaping tablespoon of batter into each cup of the prepared cupcake tins. Place a cooled miniature cupcake in the center of each cup and press it gently into the batter. Cover the cupcake with another heaping tablespoon of batter so the top and sides are completely covered and the cup is about three-quarters full. (It's okay if the top of the cupcake sticks up out of the batter a little bit—miniature cupcake tins come in different sizes, so your mini cupcakes may be slightly larger.) Bake at 350°F for 23 to 25 minutes, until the edges and tops of the cupcakes have set and the cake springs back when you gently press your finger into the top of it. Allow the cupcakes to cool in the tins for at least 10 minutes before moving to a wire rack to cool completely.

6. To frost and decorate the cupcakes, remove the vanilla cake from the cake pan, break it into pieces, and place it in a bowl or food processor. Use your hands or the food processor to break the cake up into a crumbly mixture. Set aside. To make the frosting, whip the butter for about 30 seconds with a stand mixer fitted with the whisk attachment or a hand mixer on medium speed. Add the powdered sugar, ½ cup at a time, whipping on medium-high speed until fluffy. Add the vanilla and whip until just combined. If the frosting is too thick, add the milk and whip on high for 20 seconds until the frosting is fluffy. Add the sprinkles and whip for another 20 seconds or so, until they're evenly distributed. Pipe or spread the frosting on top of the cooled cupcakes (see page 137). You can either dip the top of the cupcake into the crumbs, or dip the edges of the frosted cupcakes into the cake crumb mixture so there's a ring of cake crumbs around the edge and a circle of frosting untouched at the center of the cupcakes. That's where your birthday candles can go!

Creme Egg Cupcakes

Not only are these cupcakes decorated to look like a treat-filled basket with coconut "grass" and jelly beans, but they've also got a surprise inside, because what good is an Easter basket cupcake if it isn't full of as much candy as physically possible?

MAKES 18 CUPCAKES

CUPCAKES

¾ cup (1½ sticks) unsalted butter, at room
    temperature
1½ cups granulated sugar
3 large eggs
2 teaspoons vanilla extract
2 teaspoons baking powder
½ teaspoon baking soda
¼ teaspoon salt
2½ cups unbleached all-purpose flour
1⅓ cups whole milk
18 miniature chocolate creme eggs

FROSTING

1 cup (2 sticks) unsalted butter, at room
    temperature
2 cups powdered sugar
2 teaspoons vanilla extract
2 tablespoons whole milk, if needed
1 cup finely shredded sweetened coconut
Green food coloring
Handful of jelly beans

1. To make the cupcakes, preheat the oven to 350°F and line 2 standard muffin tins with 18 paper liners. Use a stand mixer fitted with the paddle attachment or a hand mixer on medium speed to combine the butter and sugar for 90 seconds, until fluffy. Add the eggs, one at a time, mixing in each egg completely before adding the next. Use a spatula to scrape down the side of the bowl. With the mixer on medium-low speed, add the vanilla, baking powder, baking soda, and salt. Turn the mixer up to medium-high speed and mix for an additional 30 seconds, until all the ingredients are well combined. Finally, add the flour, ½ cup at a time, alternately with the milk, ⅓ cup at a time, mixing until each addition is fully incorporated before adding the next. Scrape down the sides of the bowl again and then continue to mix the batter on medium-high speed for 30 seconds, until smooth and creamy.

2. Spoon 2 heaping tablespoons of batter into each cup in the prepared tins so they are about three-quarters full. Place a chocolate creme egg in each cup and use your finger to lightly spread the batter over it (without pushing it to the bottom of the tin—they'll sink a little on their own). Bake for about 25 minutes, until the edges and tops of the cupcakes have turned golden brown and the cake springs back when you gently press your finger into the top of it. Allow the cupcakes to cool in the tins for at least 10 minutes before moving to a wire rack to cool completely.

3. To make the frosting, whip the butter for about 30 seconds with a stand mixer fitted with the whisk attachment or a hand mixer on medium speed. Add the powdered sugar, ½ cup at a time, whipping on medium-high speed until fluffy. Add the vanilla and whip until just combined. If the frosting is too thick, add the milk and whip on high for 20 seconds until the frosting is fluffy. Put the shredded coconut in a small bowl and use a fork to mix in a few drops of green food coloring. Pipe or spread the frosting on top of the cooled cupcakes (see page 137), roll the edges of the cupcake in the dyed coconut, and then place a few jelly beans in the center.

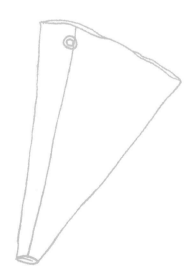

Fourth of July Apple Pie Cupcakes with Fresh Berries

With apple pies nestled in the center and red and blue berries piled on top of the fluffy vanilla frosting, of course these cupcakes are a perfect treat for your Fourth of July picnic. But there's no way they should be limited to America's birthday—anyone, anywhere will appreciate these at any time of year. For a tasty alternative, replace the apples in the pie recipe with fresh peaches.

MAKES 24 CUPCAKES

APPLE PIES

2 medium apples (I prefer Granny Smith or another tart apple)

3 tablespoons granulated sugar

2 teaspoons ground cinnamon

1 tablespoon unbleached all-purpose flour

2 (16-ounce) batches pie crust dough (your favorite recipe or store-bought, enough to make 2 two-crust pies)

CUPCAKES

¾ cup (1½ sticks) unsalted butter, at room temperature

1½ cups granulated sugar

3 large eggs

2 teaspoons vanilla extract

2 teaspoons baking powder

½ teaspoon baking soda

¼ teaspoon salt

2½ cups unbleached all-purpose flour

1⅓ cups whole milk

FROSTING

1 cup (2 sticks) unsalted butter, at room temperature

2 cups powdered sugar

Seeds from ½ vanilla bean or 2 teaspoons vanilla extract

2 tablespoons whole milk, if needed

Fresh blueberries and strawberries, for garnish

1. To make the mini apple pies, preheat the oven to 375°F and lightly grease a miniature muffin tin. Peel, core, and dice the apples into ¼-inch pieces. Place the apples, sugar, cinnamon, and flour in a bowl and stir until all the ingredients are combined and the apples are completely coated. Set aside.

2. Use a rolling pin to roll out the pie crust dough on a lightly floured smooth surface until the dough is about ⅛ inch thick. Then use a 2½-inch circular cookie cutter to cut out 48 small disks. Press half the disks into the muffin

continued on page 122 ⇒

tin and fill each cup three-quarters full with the apple mixture. Top each pie with another disk of pie dough, sealing the pies by pinching the edges of the bottom crust together with the edges of the top crust. Use a sharp knife to cut a small X into the top of each pie—this will allow some of the steam to escape as the pies bake. Bake the pies for 10 to 12 minutes, until the crust has browned. They may overflow a bit, and that's okay. They don't have to look perfect since they're going into a cupcake! Allow the pies to cool for 10 minutes in the tin and then carefully transfer them to a wire rack to finish cooling while you mix the cupcake batter.

3. To make the cupcakes, turn the oven temperature down to 350°F. Line 2 standard muffin tins with 24 paper liners. Use a stand mixer fitted with the paddle attachment or a hand mixer on medium speed to combine the butter and sugar for 90 seconds, until fluffy. Add the eggs, one at a time, mixing in each egg completely before adding the next. Use a spatula to scrape down the sides of the bowl. Then, with the mixer on medium-low speed, add the vanilla, baking powder, baking soda, and salt. Turn the mixer up to medium-high speed and mix for an additional 30 seconds, until all the ingredients are well combined. Scrape down the sides of the bowl. Finally, add the flour, ½ cup at a time, alternately with the milk, ⅓ cup

at a time, mixing until each addition is fully incorporated before adding the next. Continue to mix the batter on medium-high speed for 30 seconds, until smooth and creamy.

4. Spoon a heaping tablespoon of batter into each cup in the prepared tins. Place a cooled apple pie into the center of the batter and press it gently toward the bottom. Cover the pie with another heaping tablespoon of batter so the top and sides are completely covered and the cup is about three-quarters full. Bake at 350°F for about 25 minutes, until the edges and tops of the cupcakes have set and the cake springs back when you gently press your finger into the top of it. Allow the cupcakes to cool in the tins for at least 10 minutes before moving them to a wire rack to cool completely.

5. To make the frosting, whip the butter for about 30 seconds with a stand mixer fitted with the whisk attachment or a hand mixer on medium speed. Add the powdered sugar, ½ cup at a time, whipping on medium-high speed until fluffy. Add the vanilla seeds and whip for an additional 20 seconds or so, until combined. If the frosting is too thick, add the milk and whip on high for 20 additional seconds. Pipe or spread the frosting on top of the cooled cupcakes (see page 137) and arrange blueberries and sliced fresh strawberries on top.

Back-to-School Peanut Butter and Jelly Sandwich Cupcakes

I don't care if I am technically an "adult," a peanut butter and jelly sandwich is and always will be one of my favorite things to eat. My dad makes the best peanut butter and jelly sandwiches—he's careful to spread the peanut butter all the way to the edges of the bread on *both* slices. That's the secret. Don't be cheap with the peanut butter. Then the jelly goes on just one piece of bread (and also all the way to the edges), so the layers of the sandwich are bread, peanut butter, jelly, peanut butter, bread. You know you did it right when the jelly is just starting to drip down the sides. If your peanut butter and jelly sandwich isn't a little bit messy, you're doing it wrong.

MAKES 18 CUPCAKES

CUPCAKES

3 peanut butter and jelly sandwiches, made with the sliced bread, peanut butter, and jelly of your choice

¾ cup (1½ sticks) unsalted butter, at room temperature

1½ cups granulated sugar

3 large eggs

2 teaspoons vanilla extract

2 teaspoons baking powder

½ teaspoon baking soda

¼ teaspoon salt

2½ cups unbleached all-purpose flour

1⅓ cups whole milk

FROSTING

1 cup (2 sticks) unsalted butter, at room temperature

2 cups powdered sugar

2 teaspoons vanilla extract

2 tablespoons whole milk, if needed

Fresh banana slices, for garnish

1. To make the cupcakes, preheat the oven to 350°F and line 2 standard muffin tins with 18 paper liners. Cut each peanut butter sandwich into 6 bite-sized pieces that will fit into your tins. Set the sandwiches aside. Use a stand mixer fitted with the paddle attachment or a hand mixer on medium speed to combine the butter and sugar for 90 seconds, until fluffy. Add the eggs, one at a time, mixing in each egg completely before adding the next.

continued on page 124

Use a spatula to scrape down the sides of the bowl. Then, with the mixer on medium-low speed, add the vanilla, baking powder, baking soda, and salt. Turn the mixer up to medium-high speed and mix for an additional 30 seconds, until all the ingredients are well combined. Scrape down the sides of the bowl. Finally, add the flour, ½ cup at a time, alternately with the milk, ⅓ cup at a time, mixing until each addition is fully incorporated before adding the next. Continue to mix the batter on medium-high speed for 30 seconds, until smooth and creamy.

2. Spoon a heaping tablespoon of batter into each cup in the prepared tins. Place one bite-sized peanut butter and jelly sandwich in the center of the batter and press it gently toward the bottom. Cover the sandwich with another heaping tablespoon of batter so the top and sides are completely covered and the cup is about three-quarters full. Bake at 350°F for about 25 minutes, until the edges and tops of the cupcakes have set and the cake springs back when you gently press your finger into the top of it. Allow the cupcakes to cool in the tins for at least 10 minutes before moving to a wire rack to cool completely.

3. To make the frosting, whip the butter for about 30 seconds with a stand mixer fitted with the whisk attachment or a hand mixer on medium speed. Add the powdered sugar, ½ cup at a time, whipping on medium-high speed until fluffy. Add the vanilla and whip for an additional 20 seconds or so, until combined. If the frosting is too thick, add the milk and whip on high for 20 additional seconds. Pipe or spread the frosting on top of the cooled cupcakes (see page 137). They're extra delicious (and reminiscent of my school lunches) if you top each cupcake with a few slices of fresh banana just before serving and plate the cupcakes with a handful of Cheetos. (Okay, you can hold the Cheetos if you like.)

Bloody (Marzipan) Brain Cupcakes

Okay, so they look totally gross, but the brains are actually just tasty marzipan balls covered with some strawberry jelly—I promise they're delicious! Halloween is all about the creepy, spooky, and icky, after all, and these brain-filled cupcakes are the trick that's also a treat. This recipe makes 12 cupcakes, with some batter left over. If you'd like to make more brains, double the amount of marzipan; but because it's a pricey ingredient, I like to make some cupcakes with brains and some without, for anyone who's not a marzipan fan (or a brain-eating zombie).

MAKES 12 CUPCAKES

BRAINS
2 (7-ounce) packages marzipan
Black food gel
Powdered sugar, if needed

CUPCAKES
¾ cup (1½ sticks) unsalted butter, at room
   temperature
1½ cups granulated sugar
3 large eggs
2 teaspoons vanilla extract
2 teaspoons baking powder
½ teaspoon baking soda
¼ teaspoon salt
2½ cups unbleached all-purpose flour
1⅓ cups whole milk
⅓ cup seedless raspberry or strawberry jelly

FROSTING
1 cup (2 sticks) unsalted butter, at room
   temperature
2 cups powdered sugar
2 teaspoons vanilla extract
Seedless raspberry or strawberry jelly,
   for garnish

1. To make the brains, mix the marzipan with a couple drops of black food gel. Knead it together until the gel has been worked thoroughly into the marzipan. (You can sprinkle it with a little powdered sugar if it starts to get sticky.) Once the marzipan is the desired color, separate it into 12 small, equal-sized balls, reserving a quarter of it for later use. Form the balls into brain-shaped lumps. (It helped me to look at photos on the Internet for inspiration.) To get the lines of the brain, take some of the leftover marzipan and roll it out into a really thin snake (like you probably did with Play-Doh when you were a kid!). Gently press the thin

continued on page 126 ⇒

rope of marzipan on top of the brain-shaped balls in a wavy pattern. Set the brains aside.

2. To make the cupcakes, preheat the oven to 350°F and line a standard muffin tin with 12 paper liners. Use a stand mixer fitted with the paddle attachment or a hand mixer on medium speed to combine the butter and sugar for 90 seconds, until fluffy. Add the eggs, one at a time, mixing in each egg completely before adding the next. Use a spatula to scrape down the side of the bowl. With the mixer on medium-low speed, add the vanilla, baking powder, baking soda, and salt. Turn the mixer up to medium-high speed and mix for an additional 30 seconds, until all the ingredients are well combined. Finally, add the flour, ½ cup at a time, alternately with the milk, ⅓ cup at a time, mixing until each addition is fully incorporated before adding the next. Scrape down the sides of the bowl again and then continue to mix the batter on medium-high speed for 30 seconds, until smooth and creamy.

3. Spoon 2 heaping tablespoons of batter into each cup in the prepared tin so they are about half full. Place a brain in each cup and put a small spoonful of jelly on top of that. Top with a small spoonful of batter and use your finger to lightly spread the batter over the brains and jelly so they're completely covered. (Be careful not to push the brains to the bottom of the tin—they'll sink a little on their own.) Bake for about 25 minutes, until the edges and tops of the cupcakes have turned golden brown and the cake springs back when you gently press your finger into the top of it. Allow the cupcakes to cool in the tin for at least 10 minutes before moving to a wire rack to cool completely.

4. To make the frosting, whip the butter for about 30 seconds with a stand mixer fitted with the whisk attachment or a hand mixer on medium speed. Add the powdered sugar, ½ cup at a time, whipping on medium-high speed until fluffy. Add the vanilla and whip until just combined. If the frosting is too thick, add the milk and whip on high for 20 seconds until the frosting is fluffy. If you'd like, slightly warm some extra jelly in the microwave on low heat and drizzle it over the top of the cupcakes for a creepy (but tasty!) finish.

Reese's Pieces Halloween Brownie Bites

Like the conversation heart brownie bites found earlier in this chapter, these brownies can be made with one bowl and less than an hour's time if you skip the frosting. But Halloween is not the time to be counting calories, so I like to whip up some peanut butter frosting to go on top (see page 27).

MAKES 36 MINI BROWNIE CUPCAKES

BROWNIES

4 ounces unsweetened chocolate, broken or chopped into small pieces

¾ cup (1½ sticks) unsalted butter

2 cups granulated sugar

3 large eggs

½ teaspoon salt

1 teaspoon vanilla extract

1 cup unbleached all-purpose flour

¾ cup candy-coated peanut butter candy, such as Reese's Pieces, plus more for garnish

FROSTING

1 cup (2 sticks) unsalted butter, at room temperature

½ cup smooth or crunchy peanut butter

2 cups powdered sugar

2 tablespoons whole milk, if needed

1. To make the brownies, preheat the oven to 350°F and line 2 miniature muffin tins with 36 paper liners. Place the chocolate and butter in a medium microwave-safe bowl and microwave on high for 90 seconds, stopping halfway through to stir the butter and chocolate together. After 90 seconds, continue to stir the butter and chocolate until all the chocolate chunks have melted completely into the butter. (If you microwave any longer, you risk burning the chocolate, so it's best to be patient and let the chocolate melt slowly while you stir.) Using a wooden spoon, stir in the granulated sugar. It will be thick and grainy, and the sugar should be distributed evenly. Next, stir in the eggs one at a time until the mixture is smooth. Add the salt and vanilla and stir for an additional 20 seconds, until they're both incorporated. Mix in the flour until just combined and then stir in ¾ cup of the Reese's Pieces.

continued on page 128 ➡

2. Using a 1-inch cookie scoop, spoon the brownie batter into the tins, so the cups are about three-quarters full. Bake for about 20 minutes, or until the brownies have set and a toothpick inserted into the center of a brownie comes out clean. (Take care not to overbake or your brownies could be quite dry.) Allow the brownies to cool in the tins for 10 minutes before transferring to a wire rack to finish cooling.

3. To make the frosting, whip the butter and peanut butter together for about 30 seconds with a stand mixer fitted with the whisk attachment or a hand mixer on medium speed. Add the powdered sugar, ½ cup at a time, whipping on medium-high speed until fluffy. If the frosting is too thick, add the milk and whip on high for 20 seconds, until the frosting is fluffy. Pipe or spread the frosting on top of the cooled brownie bites (see page 137) and top with a piece of candy.

Pumpkin Pie Cupcakes with Cinnamon Cream Cheese Frosting

This has been, hands down, the most popular *Bake It in a Cupcake* creation to date. That's not very surprising when you consider that pumpkin pie is the second most popular pie in America.

To save time, you can make the miniature pies up to 2 days in advance—just store them in the refrigerator until you're ready to make the cupcakes. The pies can also be prepared quickly with premade pie crust—as I've said, there's no shame in taking shortcuts.

Though they sound like the perfect Thanksgiving dessert (and they are), I've done plenty of research and am happy to confirm that they taste just as good at any time of year.

MAKES 24 CUPCAKES

PUMPKIN PIES

1 (16-ounce) batch pie crust dough (your favorite recipe or store-bought, enough to make 2 one-crust pies)

1 (15-ounce) can pumpkin pie filling, made as directed on the can

CUPCAKES

¾ cup (1½ sticks) unsalted butter, at room temperature

8 ounces cream cheese, at room temperature

1½ cups granulated sugar

3 large eggs

2 teaspoons vanilla extract

2 teaspoons baking powder

½ teaspoon baking soda

½ teaspoon salt

2½ cups unbleached all-purpose flour

1⅓ cups whole milk

FROSTING

2 tablespoons heavy cream or whole milk

1 cup cinnamon chips (see Baker's tip, page 132)

1 cup (2 sticks) unsalted butter, at room temperature

8 ounces cream cheese, at room temperature

2 cups powdered sugar

DECORATION

½ cup granulated sugar, for garnish

2 teaspoons ground cinnamon, for garnish

1. To make the mini pumpkin pies, preheat the oven to 425°F and lightly grease a 24-cup miniature muffin tin. Use a rolling pin to roll out the pie crust dough on a lightly floured smooth surface until the dough is about ⅛ inch thick. Then use a 2½-inch circular cookie cutter to cut out 24 small disks. Ball up the scraps of dough and wrap in plastic wrap for later use.

2. Press the dough circles into each cup in the prepared tin and fill three-quarters full with the prepared pumpkin pie filling. Keep in mind the pumpkin pie filling will expand a bit while baking. Bake the pies for about 7 minutes. With the pies still in the oven, turn the oven down to 350°F and bake for an additional 7 to 10 minutes, until the edges of the crust have browned and the pumpkin pie filling no longer jiggles when you gently shake the tin. Allow the pies to cool for 5 minutes in the tin and then carefully transfer them to a wire rack to finish cooling while you mix the cupcake batter.

3. To make the cupcakes, line 2 standard muffin tins with 24 paper liners. Use a stand mixer fitted with the paddle attachment or a hand mixer on medium speed to combine the butter and cream cheese for about 90 seconds, until smooth. Add the sugar and mix on medium-high until fluffy. Add the eggs, one at a time, mixing in each egg completely before adding the next. With the mixer on medium speed, add the vanilla, baking powder, baking soda, and salt. Finally, add the flour, ½ cup at a time, alternately with the milk, ⅓ cup at a time, mixing until each addition is fully incorporated before adding the next. Continue to mix the batter on medium-high speed for 30 seconds, until smooth and creamy.

4. Spoon a heaping tablespoon of batter into each cup in the prepared tins. Place a cooled pumpkin pie into the center of the batter and press it gently. You don't want the pie to touch the bottom of the tin. Cover the pies with another heaping tablespoon of batter so the top and sides of the mini pie are completely covered and the cup is about three-quarters full. Bake for 25 minutes, until the edges and tops of the cupcakes have turned golden brown and the cake springs back when you gently press your finger into the top of it. Allow the cupcakes to cool in the tins for at least 10 minutes before moving to a wire rack to cool completely.

5. To make the frosting, melt the cream and cinnamon chips together in a microwave in a small microwave-safe bowl for about 45 seconds on high. Stir the mixture until all the chips have melted and place in the fridge while you prepare the rest of the frosting. Using a stand mixer fitted with a paddle attachment or a hand mixer, cream together the butter and cream cheese on medium-high speed for about 30 seconds, until smooth. Whip in the powdered sugar, ½ cup at a time, until the mixture is fluffy. Finally, with the mixer on low, drizzle in the cinnamon chip mixture. (Make sure it has cooled a bit—if it's too hot, it will melt the frosting.) Spread or swirl a generous helping of the frosting onto the cupcakes using a spatula or pastry bag. (See page 137).

continued on page 132 ➡

6. Put the leftover pie crust scraps to good use by making cinnamon-sugar decorations. Mix the sugar and cinnamon in a small bowl. Use a rolling pin to roll out the reserved ball of dough onto a lightly floured smooth surface until it's about ⅛ inch thick, then cut out quarter-sized circles with a small cookie cutter or frosting tip. Place them on a baking sheet, sprinkle them with a little bit of the cinnamon and sugar mixture, and bake for about 10 minutes at 350°F, until they're golden brown. Once they're cool, put one on top of each of the cupcakes and serve.

BAKER'S TIP

Can't find cinnamon baking chips at your local market? You can make a delicious alternative by tossing 1 cup white chocolate chips with 2 teaspoons ground cinnamon. Then follow the frosting recipe as directed.

Caramelized Yams in Pecan Cupcakes with Toasted Marshmallows

One of the greatest Thanksgiving side dishes is now in a cupcake. If your family makes this dish with sweet potatoes instead of yams, feel free to switch them in for the yams in this recipe. You could also serve these cupcakes without the marshmallow topping (try them with the spiced buttercream on page 8), but I consider marshmallows to be one of the four food groups, so I include them whenever possible.

MAKES 20 CUPCAKES

YAM FILLING

2 medium yams, peeled and cut into $\frac{1}{4}$-inch
    cubes (about 2 cups)
2 cups water
6 tablespoons ($\frac{3}{4}$ stick) butter
$\frac{1}{4}$ cup brown sugar, packed
2 teaspoons ground allspice
Pinch of salt

CUPCAKES

$\frac{3}{4}$ cup ($1\frac{1}{2}$ sticks) unsalted butter, at room
    temperature
$1\frac{1}{2}$ cups granulated sugar
3 large eggs
2 teaspoons vanilla extract
2 teaspoons baking powder
$\frac{1}{2}$ teaspoon baking soda
$\frac{1}{4}$ teaspoon salt
$2\frac{1}{2}$ cups unbleached all-purpose flour
$1\frac{1}{3}$ cups whole milk
1 cup pecans, finely chopped
3 cups mini marshmallows

1. To make the yam filling, place the yams in a microwave-safe bowl, pour in the water, and microwave on high for 7 minutes, until the yams are barely fork-tender. Drain the liquid and set aside. Mix together the butter, brown sugar, allspice, and salt in a medium saucepan over medium-high heat. Once the butter is melted and the sugar is dissolved, add the yams and stir until they're completely coated. Turn the heat down to medium and simmer for a few minutes, allowing the yams to caramelize. Give it a taste to make sure you don't want more spices or salt. Then remove the yams from the heat and allow them to cool.

2. To make the cupcakes, preheat the oven to 350°F and line 2 standard muffin tins with 20 paper liners. Use a stand mixer fitted with the paddle attachment or a hand mixer on medium speed to combine the butter and sugar for 90 seconds, until fluffy. Add the eggs, one at a time, mixing in each egg completely before

adding the next. Use a spatula to scrape down the sides of the bowl. Then, with the mixer on medium-low speed, add the vanilla, baking powder, baking soda, and salt. Turn the mixer up to medium-high speed and mix for an additional 30 seconds, until all the ingredients are well combined. Finally, add the flour, ½ cup at a time, alternately with the milk, ⅓ cup at a time, mixing until each addition is fully incorporated before adding the next. Scrape down the sides of the bowl again and continue to mix the batter on medium-high speed for 30 seconds. Add the pecans and use a spatula to fold them in until just combined. The mixture will be creamy and evenly flecked with pecans.

3. Spoon 2 heaping tablespoons of batter into each cup in the prepared tins so they're two-thirds full. Spoon a heaping teaspoon of the yam mixture (okay, maybe a tiny bit more) over the batter. Top the yams with a teaspoon of batter, but you don't have to completely cover all the yams. Bake for about 25 minutes, or until the edges of the cupcakes have started to turn golden brown and the cake around the

sides of the yam mixture is set (it'll bounce back when you gently press your finger into it).

4. As soon as the cupcakes are finished baking, remove them from the oven and immediately top each hot cupcake with a small handful of mini marshmallows. This can be tricky—the marshmallows will want to roll off, so pile them on while the cake is hot so they melt a little and stick to the top of the cupcake. You'll have to work. But don't worry about getting all the marshmallows on there—you can pile on a few more once you have the initial layer in place. Once all the cupcakes have a layer of marshmallows on top (feel free to pile on a few more marshmallows, if you'd like—I always do, because why not?), turn on the oven broiler and place the cupcake tins under the broiler for about 1 minute. Do not walk away from the oven. You just want the marshmallows to begin to toast, and it will happen quickly. Remove the cupcakes from the oven and let them rest in the tins for about 10 minutes. Then transfer to a wire rack and allow them to finish cooling in the fridge so the marshmallow topping doesn't melt away. Bring to room temperature before serving.

Gingerbread House Cupcakes (with Gingerbread Men Inside)

If you like making gingerbread man cookies during the holiday season, you should try something new this year: Bake a gingerbread man into a cupcake. For best results, use a gingerbread cookie that is at least ½ inch thick and 2 or 3 inches tall. (I had great success with Franz Gingerbread Boys.) Once your gingerbread man is safely nestled inside, you can build up your candy house by using some graham crackers for the roof and adding frosting and lots of colorful candy.

If you plan on using a lot of frosting as decoration—to make icicles or snow-covered rooftops—you should double the frosting recipe below to ensure you have enough.

MAKES 18 CUPCAKES

CUPCAKES

¾ cup (1½ sticks) unsalted butter, at room temperature
1½ cups granulated sugar
3 large eggs
2 teaspoons vanilla extract
2 teaspoons baking powder
½ teaspoon baking soda
¼ teaspoon salt
2½ cups unbleached all-purpose flour
1⅓ cups whole milk
18 small gingerbread men cookies

FROSTING

2 sticks (1 cup) unsalted butter, at room temperature
2 cups powdered sugar
36 graham cracker squares
Assorted candies and sprinkles for decoration

1. To make the cupcakes, preheat the oven to 350°F and line 2 standard muffin tins with 18 paper liners. Use a stand mixer fitted with the paddle attachment or a hand mixer on medium speed to combine the butter and sugar for 90 seconds, until fluffy. Add the eggs, one at a time, mixing in each egg completely before adding the next. Use a spatula to scrape down the side of the bowl. With the mixer on medium-low speed, add the vanilla, baking powder, baking soda, and salt. Turn the mixer up to medium-high speed and mix for an additional 30 seconds, until all the ingredients are well combined. Finally, add the flour, ½ cup at a time, alternately with the milk, ⅓ cup at a time, mixing until each addition is fully incorporated before adding the next. Scrape down the sides of the bowl again and then continue to mix the batter on medium-high speed for 30 seconds, until smooth and creamy.

2. Pour the batter into each cup in the prepared tins so they are about three-quarters full. Place one gingerbread man cookie in each cup, so he's standing up—feet at the bottom of the cup, head above the batter. Bake for about 25 minutes, until the edges and tops of the cupcakes have turned golden brown and the cake springs back when you gently press your finger into the top of it. Allow the cupcakes to cool in the tins for at least 10 minutes before moving to a wire rack to cool completely.

3. To make the frosting, whip the butter for about 30 seconds with a stand mixer fitted with the whisk attachment or a hand mixer on medium speed. Add the powdered sugar, ½ cup at a time, whipping on medium-high speed until fluffy. Add the vanilla and whip until just combined. If the frosting is too thick, add the milk and whip on high for 20 seconds, until the frosting is fluffy. Pipe or spread the frosting onto the cupcakes. Press 2 graham cracker squares into the frosting at an angle, to form the roof, and pipe or spread some frosting at the peak to keep the crackers together. Pipe some frosting icicles on the edges of the graham crackers or use little dabs of frosting to stick pieces of candy onto the roof—decorate however you'd like.

BAKER'S TIP

If you don't have a pastry bag, you can still decorate like the pros by using a clean resealable plastic bag. Fill the bag two-thirds of the way full and twist the top of the bag closed while squeezing out the excess air. Use a pair of scissors to snip off one of the corners, and use as you would any pastry bag. Fancy!

Eggnog Pudding Pie Cupcakes with Cranberry Frosting

This might be one of the most involved recipes in this book, but don't let that scare you. If you don't feel like making fresh cranberry sauce, you can absolutely substitute canned—I used Ocean Spray and prefer to use sauce over jelly, which still has chunks of berries in it. You can also make the eggnog pudding pies a day or two in advance to break up the workload, although doing that will require some impressive willpower. I'm an eggnog junkie, and if these pies were in my possession they wouldn't last 2 hours, let alone 24.

MAKES 22 CUPCAKES

EGGNOG PUDDING PIES
1 (16-ounce) batch pie crust dough (your favorite recipe or store-bought)
1 (4.6-ounce) box of vanilla cook-and-serve pudding
3 cups eggnog

CUPCAKES
1½ sticks (¾ cup) unsalted butter, at room temperature
1½ cups granulated sugar
3 large eggs
2 teaspoons vanilla extract
2 teaspoons baking powder
½ teaspoon baking soda
½ teaspoon salt
2 ½ cups unbleached flour
1⅓ cups whole milk

FROSTING
2 cups fresh cranberries
2 tablespoons granulated sugar
1 cup water
1 cup (2 sticks) unsalted butter, at room temperature
2 cups powdered sugar

1. To make the pie shells, preheat the oven to 375°F and lightly grease 22 cups in a miniature muffin tin. Use a rolling pin to roll out the pie crust dough onto a lightly floured smooth surface so the dough is about ⅛ inch thick and then use a 2½-inch circular cookie cutter to cut out 22 small disks. Press the dough disks into the tin and bake for 7 to 10 minutes, until the crusts turn golden brown. Remove them from the oven and allow them to cool completely in the tin. Turn the oven down to 350°F.

2. To make the pudding filling, whisk the pudding mix and eggnog together in a medium saucepan over medium-high heat. Continue to whisk every couple of minutes, until the mixture starts to boil (it will take about 10 minutes). Once the mixture is boiling and starting to get thick, pour the pudding into a heatproof bowl and lay a sheet of plastic wrap directly on the surface of the pudding (this keeps a pudding "skin" from forming). Place it in the refrigerator so it can cool while you make the cupcakes.

3. To make the cupcakes, line 2 standard muffin tins with 22 paper liners. Use a stand mixer fitted with the paddle attachment or a hand mixer on medium speed to combine the butter and sugar for 90 seconds, until it is fluffy. Add the eggs, one at a time, mixing in each egg completely before adding the next. With the mixer on medium-low speed, add the vanilla, baking powder, baking soda, and salt. Turn the mixer up to medium-high speed and mix for an additional 30 seconds, until all the ingredients are well combined. Finally, add the flour, ½ cup at a time, alternately with the milk, ⅓ cup at a time, mixing until each addition is fully incorporated before adding the next. Continue to mix the batter on medium-high speed another 30 seconds, until smooth and creamy.

4. Remove the pudding from the refrigerator and spoon a heaping tablespoon into each of the pie shells so they're full but not overflowing. Spoon a heaping tablespoon of batter into each cup in the prepared tins. Place a pudding pie into the center of the batter and press it gently. You don't want the pie to touch the bottom of the tin. Cover the pies with another heaping tablespoon of batter so the top and sides of the mini pie are completely covered and the cup is about three-quarters full. Bake for 25 minutes, until the edges and tops of the cupcakes have turned golden brown and the cake springs back when you gently press your finger into the top of it. Allow the cupcakes to cool in the tins for at least 10 minutes before moving to a wire rack to cool completely.

5. To make the frosting, combine the cranberries, sugar, and water in a small saucepan over medium heat. Bring the mixture to a boil and then stir every few minutes for 12 minutes, until the cranberries start to pop and the mixture begins to thicken (it'll splatter a bit, so be careful). Once all (or most) of the berries have popped, remove the mixture from the heat. Place a fine-mesh strainer over a medium bowl and press the cranberry mixture through the strainer. In the bowl you will be left with cranberry jelly. Allow the cranberry jelly to cool in the refrigerator while you prepare to finish the frosting.

continued on page 140 ➡

6. Whip the butter for about 30 seconds with a stand mixer fitted with the whisk attachment or a hand mixer on medium speed. Add the powdered sugar, ½ cup at a time, whipping on medium-high speed until fluffy. With the mixer on medium speed, slowly add the cooled cranberry jelly, a heaping spoonful at a time. Give the frosting a taste to see if you need to add more sugar (some like their cranberry sauce tart; others like it sweet) and add as necessary. Pipe or spread the frosting on top of the cooled cupcakes (see page 137).

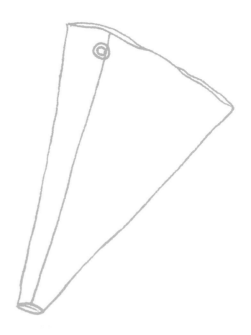

Candy Cane Brownies

These decadent brownie bites have a Candy Cane Hershey Kiss baked into the center, making for a sweet, peppermint surprise. Top them with red striped vanilla frosting and some chunky sanding sugar or crushed candy cane pieces and they become a winter wonderland in one little brownie.

MAKES 36 MINIATURE BROWNIES

BROWNIES

4 ounces unsweetened chocolate, broken or
    chopped into small pieces
¾ cup (1½ sticks) unsalted butter
2 cups granulated sugar
3 large eggs
½ teaspoon salt
1 teaspoon vanilla extract
1 cup unbleached all-purpose flour
36 Candy Cane Hershey Kiss candies, unwrapped

FROSTING

40 peppermint candies or 8 candy canes
2 sticks (1 cup) unsalted butter, at room
    temperature
2 cups powdered sugar
2 teaspoons vanilla extract
2 tablespoons whole milk, if needed
Red food gel
Crushed candy cane pieces, or sanding sugar,
    for garnish

1. To make the brownies, preheat the oven to 350°F and line 2 miniature muffin tins with 36 paper liners. Place the chocolate and butter in a medium microwave-safe bowl and microwave on high for 90 seconds, stopping halfway through to stir the butter and chocolate together. After 90 seconds, continue to stir the butter and chocolate until all the chocolate chunks have completely melted into the butter. (If you microwave any longer, you risk burning the chocolate, so it's best to be patient and let the chocolate melt slowly while you stir.) Using a wooden spoon, stir in the granulated sugar. It will be thick and grainy, and the sugar should be distributed evenly throughout. Next, stir in the eggs one at a time until the mixture is smooth. Add the salt and vanilla and stir for an additional 20 seconds, until they're both incorporated. Finally, mix in the flour until just combined, taking care not to overstir.

2. Using a 1-inch cookie scoop, spoon the brownie batter into each cup in the tins so they're about three-quarters full. Press one candy kiss into each cupcake tin and cover with a little more brownie batter so the candy kiss is covered. (The tip of the kiss may stick out of the brownie batter—that's okay.) Bake for 23 minutes, or until the brownies have set. (Take care not to overbake or your brownies could be quite dry.) Allow the brownies to cool in the tins for 10 minutes before transferring them to a wire rack to finish cooling.

3. To make the frosting, place the candy in a resealable plastic bag and use a rolling pin or meat tenderizer to crush them into very small pieces (but not a fine powder). Set the crushed candy aside. Whip the butter for about 30 seconds with a stand mixer fitted with the whisk attachment or a hand mixer on medium speed. Add the powdered sugar, ½ cup at a time, whipping on medium-high speed until fluffy. Add the vanilla and whip until just combined. If the frosting is too thick, add the milk and whip on high for 20 seconds, until the frosting is fluffy.

4. To make the candy cane stripes, use a clean, small paintbrush to paint a few stripes of red food gel straight up the insides of a pastry bag fitted with the desired decorative tip. Fill the pastry bag with the frosting and pipe a small dollop onto the brownies as usual (see page 137). The frosting will come out with red stripes! Finish the cupcakes with crushed candy cane pieces. (If you don't have candy canes, you can use sanding sugar, which is chunkier than granulated sugar—it'll give the brownies a sweet, "icy" finish.)

YOUR TURN: BUILDING YOUR OWN
BAKE IT IN A CUPCAKE CREATION

Something happened to my brain when I first started baking things into other things. I couldn't turn it off. My mind was reeling, day and night, with all the different flavor combinations I wanted to try, and it's very likely the same thing will happen to you. As you begin your *Bake It in a Cupcake* journey, use these pages to jot down your ideas before you forget them. Or, if you want to try something new but aren't yet feeling inspired, here's a great place to start. Just write down some of your favorites kinds of cakes in the first column (chocolate, vanilla, spice, cream cheese, etc.), then write down your favorite pastries, candies, and fruits in the second column. Start mixing and matching your ingredients with different kinds of frostings and toppings and you'll be crafting your own stuffed creations before you can say "team buttercream."

CAKE FLAVOR	THE SURPRISE INSIDE	WHAT GOES ON TOP

CAKE FLAVOR	THE SURPRISE INSIDE	WHAT GOES ON TOP

CAKE FLAVOR	THE SURPRISE INSIDE	WHAT GOES ON TOP

CAKE FLAVOR	THE SURPRISE INSIDE	WHAT GOES ON TOP

CAKE FLAVOR	THE SURPRISE INSIDE	WHAT GOES ON TOP

ACKNOWLEDGMENTS

A goofy baking experiment went from a weekend hobby to a personal obsession to a blog to a book deal within a year. For that I would like to thank/blame: my parents, Bill and Sue, and my sister, Katie, for, well, everything; Robby MacDonell for still marrying me when I decided it was totally possible to plan a wedding, bake hundreds (thousands?) of cupcakes, and write a cookbook all at the same time; Renee Zuckerbrot for making the terrifying process of writing a book proposal, pitching it to publishers, and signing a contract feel effortless and even fun; Jean Lucas and everyone at Andrews McMeel Publishing for knowing the world is still not done with cupcakes (and it probably never will be); Clare Barboza, Helene Dujardin, and Kate Basart for making my cupcakes look better than they've ever looked before (that sounds kind of dirty, actually); Paul Constant for reminding me not to take it too seriously; all my coworkers at *The Stranger* who bravely ate dozens upon dozens of these experimental cupcakes without complaining even once; Jessie Oleson, aka CakeSpy, for being the very first person to write kind words about Bake It in a Cake, but more importantly for loving butter even more than I do; Zack Bolotin at Porchlight Coffee for hosting bake sales even though I never showed up on time; and, of course, the biggest, sweetest, most butter-stuffed and sincere thanks to anyone who has come to the bake sales, baked any of the recipes, sent me photos of their own *Bake It in a Cupcake* inventions, and/or recognized how ridiculous *Bake It in a Cupcake* really is and loved it anyway. THANK YOU.

METRIC CONVERSIONS AND EQUIVALENTS

METRIC CONVERSION FORMULAS

TO CONVERT	MULTIPLY
Ounces to grams	Ounces by 28.35
Pounds to kilograms	Pounds by .454
Teaspoons to milliliters	Teaspoons by 4.93
Tablespoons to milliliters	Tablespoons by 14.79
Fluid ounces to milliliters	Fluid ounces by 29.57
Cups to milliliters	Cups by 236.59
Cups to liters	Cups by .236
Pints to liters	Pints by .473
Quarts to liters	Quarts by .946
Gallons to liters	Gallons by 3.785
Inches to centimeters	Inches by 2.54

APPROXIMATE METRIC EQUIVALENTS

VOLUME	
¼ teaspoon	1 milliliter
½ teaspoon	2.5 milliliters
¾ teaspoon	4 milliliters
1 teaspoon	5 milliliters
1¼ teaspoon	6 milliliters
1½ teaspoon	7.5 milliliters
1¾ teaspoon	8.5 milliliters
2 teaspoons	10 milliliters
1 tablespoon (½ fluid ounce)	15 milliliters
2 tablespoons (1 fluid ounce)	30 milliliters
¼ cup	60 milliliters
⅓ cup	80 milliliters

½ cup (4 fluid ounces)	120 milliliters
⅔ cup	160 milliliters
¾ cup	180 milliliters
1 cup (8 fluid ounces)	240 milliliters
1¼ cups	300 milliliters
1½ cups (12 fluid ounces)	360 milliliters
1⅔ cups	400 milliliters
2 cups (1 pint)	460 milliliters
3 cups	700 milliliters
4 cups (1 quart)	.95 liter
1 quart plus ¼ cup	1 liter
4 quarts (1 gallon)	3.8 liters

WEIGHT	
¼ ounce	7 grams
½ ounce	14 grams
¾ ounce	21 grams
1 ounce	28 grams
1¼ ounces	35 grams
1½ ounces	42.5 grams
1⅔ ounces	45 grams
2 ounces	57 grams
3 ounces	85 grams
4 ounces (¼ pound)	113 grams
5 ounces	142 grams
6 ounces	170 grams
7 ounces	198 grams
8 ounces (½ pound)	227 grams
16 ounces (1 pound)	454 grams
35.25 ounces (2.2 pounds)	1 kilogram

LENGTH	
⅛ inch	3 millimeters
¼ inch	6 millimeters
½ inch	1 ¼ centimeters
1 inch	2 ½ centimeters
2 inches	5 centimeters
2½ inches	6 centimeters
4 inches	10 centimeters
5 inches	13 centimeters
6 inches	15 ¼ centimeters
12 inches (1 foot)	30 centimeters

OVEN TEMPERATURES

DESCRIPTION	FAHRENHEIT	CELSIUS	BRITISH GAS MARK
Very cool	200˚	95˚	0
Very cool	225˚	110˚	¼
Very cool	250˚	120˚	½
Cool	275˚	135˚	1
Cool	300˚	150˚	2
Warm	325˚	165˚	3
Moderate	350˚	175˚	4
Moderately hot	375˚	190˚	5
Fairly hot	400˚	200˚	6
Hot	425˚	220˚	7
Very hot	450˚	230˚	8
Very hot	475˚	245˚	9

*To convert Fahrenheit to Celsius, subtract 32 from Fahrenheit, multiply the result by 5, then divide by 9.

COMMON INGREDIENTS AND THEIR APPROXIMATE EQUIVALENTS

1 cup uncooked rice = 225 grams	
1 cup all-purpose flour = 140 grams	
1 stick butter (4 ounces • ½ cup • 8 tablespoons) = 110 grams	
1 cup butter (8 ounces • 2 sticks • 16 tablespoons) = 220 grams	
1 cup brown sugar, firmly packed = 225 grams	
1 cup granulated sugar = 200 grams	

Information compiled from a variety of sources, including *Recipes into Type* by Joan Whitman and Dolores Simon (Newton, MA: Biscuit Books, 2000); *The New Food Lover's Companion* by Sharon Tyler Herbst (Hauppauge, NY: Barron's, 1995); and *Rosemary Brown's Big Kitchen Instruction Book* (Kansas City, MO: Andrews McMeel, 1998).

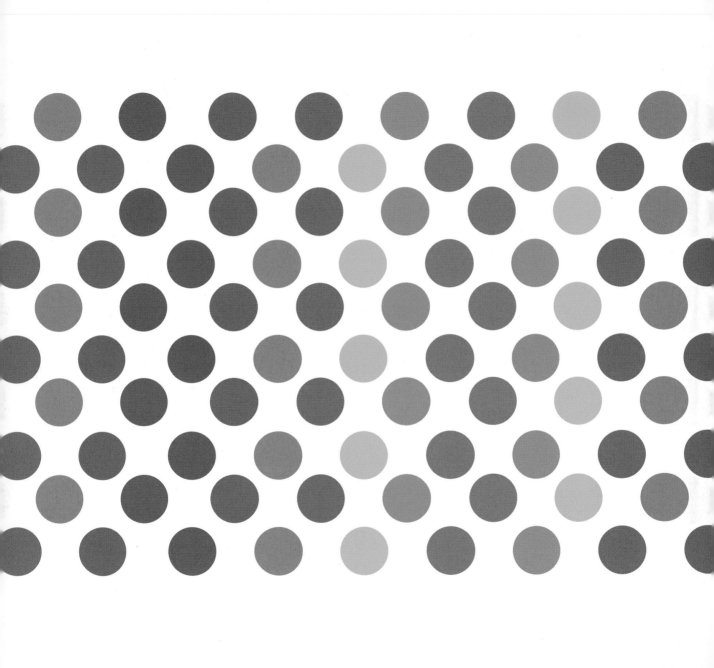

INDEX

BAKE IT IN A CUPCAKE